D0812368

SQA

Official

SQA
Past Papers
WITH ANSWERS

Higher
Modern
Studies

2010–2014

HODDER
GIBSON
AN HACHETTE UK COMPANY

Hodder Gibson is grateful to the copyright holders, as credited on the final page of the Question Section, for permission to use their material. Every effort has been made to trace the copyright holders and to obtain their permission for the use of copyright material. Hodder Gibson will be happy to receive information allowing us to rectify any error or omission in future editions.

Hachette UK's policy is to use papers that are natural, renewable and recyclable products and made from wood grown in sustainable forests. The logging and manufacturing processes are expected to conform to the environmental regulations of the country of origin.

Orders: please contact Bookpoint Ltd, 130 Park Drive, Abingdon, Oxon OX14 4SE. Telephone: (44) 01235 827720. Fax: (44) 01235 400454.

Lines are open 9.00–5.00, Monday to Saturday, with a 24-hour message answering service. Visit our website at www.hoddereducation.co.uk. Hodder Gibson can be contacted direct on: Tel: 0141 848 1609; Fax: 0141 889 6315; email: hoddergibson@hodder.co.uk

This collection first published in 2014 by

Hodder Gibson, an imprint of Hodder Education,

An Hachette UK Company

2a Christie Street

Paisley PA1 1NB

BrightRED   Hodder Gibson is grateful to Bright Red Publishing Ltd for collaborative work in preparation of this book and all
PUBLISHING   SQA Past Paper, National 5 and Higher for CfE Model Paper titles 2014.

Typeset by PDQ Digital Media Solutions Ltd, Bungay, Suffolk NR35 1BY

Printed in the UK

A catalogue record for this title is available from the British Library

ISBN 978-1-4718-3686-2

3 2 1

2015 2014

Introduction

Study Skills – what you need to know to pass exams!

Pause for thought

Many students might skip quickly through a page like this. After all, we all know how to revise. Do you really though?

Think about this:

"IF YOU ALWAYS DO WHAT YOU ALWAYS DO, YOU WILL ALWAYS GET WHAT YOU HAVE ALWAYS GOT."

Do you like the grades you get? Do you want to do better? If you get full marks in your assessment, then that's great! Change nothing! This section is just to help you get that little bit better than you already are.

There are two main parts to the advice on offer here. The first part highlights fairly obvious things but which are also very important. The second part makes suggestions about revision that you might not have thought about but which WILL help you.

Part 1

DOH! It's so obvious but …

Start revising in good time

Don't leave it until the last minute – this will make you panic.

Make a revision timetable that sets out work time AND play time.

Sleep and eat!

Obvious really, and very helpful. Avoid arguments or stressful things too – even games that wind you up. You need to be fit, awake and focused!

Know your place!

Make sure you know exactly **WHEN and WHERE** your exams are.

Know your enemy!

Make sure you know what to expect in the exam.

How is the paper structured?

How much time is there for each question?

What types of question are involved?

Which topics seem to come up time and time again?

Which topics are your strongest and which are your weakest?

Are all topics compulsory or are there choices?

Learn by DOING!

There is no substitute for past papers and practice papers – they are simply essential! Tackling this collection of papers and answers is exactly the right thing to be doing as your exams approach.

Part 2

People learn in different ways. Some like low light, some bright. Some like early morning, some like evening / night. Some prefer warm, some prefer cold. But everyone uses their BRAIN and the brain works when it is active. Passive learning – sitting gazing at notes – is the most INEFFICIENT way to learn anything. Below you will find tips and ideas for making your revision more effective and maybe even more enjoyable. What follows gets your brain active, and active learning works!

Activity 1 – Stop and review

Step 1

When you have done no more than 5 minutes of revision reading STOP!

Step 2

Write a heading in your own words which sums up the topic you have been revising.

Step 3

Write a summary of what you have revised in no more than two sentences. Don't fool yourself by saying, "I know it, but I cannot put it into words". That just means you don't know it well enough. If you cannot write your summary, revise that section again, knowing that you must write a summary at the end of it. Many of you will have notebooks full of blue/black ink writing. Many of the pages will not be especially attractive or memorable so try to liven them up a bit with colour as you are reviewing and rewriting. **This is a great memory aid, and memory is the most important thing.**

Activity 2 — Use technology!

Why should everything be written down? Have you thought about "mental" maps, diagrams, cartoons and colour to help you learn? And rather than write down notes, why not record your revision material?

What about having a text message revision session with friends? Keep in touch with them to find out how and what they are revising and share ideas and questions.

Why not make a video diary where you tell the camera what you are doing, what you think you have learned and what you still have to do? No one has to see or hear it, but the process of having to organise your thoughts in a formal way to explain something is a very important learning practice.

Be sure to make use of electronic files. You could begin to summarise your class notes. Your typing might be slow, but it will get faster and the typed notes will be easier to read than the scribbles in your class notes. Try to add different fonts and colours to make your work stand out. You can easily Google relevant pictures, cartoons and diagrams which you can copy and paste to make your work more attractive and **MEMORABLE**.

Activity 3 – This is it. Do this and you will know lots!

Step 1

In this task you must be very honest with yourself! Find the SQA syllabus for your subject (www.sqa.org.uk). Look at how it is broken down into main topics called MANDATORY knowledge. That means stuff you MUST know.

Step 2

BEFORE you do ANY revision on this topic, write a list of everything that you already know about the subject. It might be quite a long list but you only need to write it once. It shows you all the information that is already in your long-term memory so you know what parts you do not need to revise!

Step 3

Pick a chapter or section from your book or revision notes. Choose a fairly large section or a whole chapter to get the most out of this activity.

With a buddy, use Skype, Facetime, Twitter or any other communication you have, to play the game "If this is the answer, what is the question?". For example, if you are revising Geography and the answer you provide is "meander", your buddy would have to make up a question like "What is the word that describes a feature of a river where it flows slowly and bends often from side to side?".

Make up 10 "answers" based on the content of the chapter or section you are using. Give this to your buddy to solve while you solve theirs.

Step 4

Construct a wordsearch of at least 10 X 10 squares. You can make it as big as you like but keep it realistic. Work together with a group of friends. Many apps allow you to make wordsearch puzzles online. The words and phrases can go in any direction and phrases can be split. Your puzzle must only contain facts linked to the topic you are revising. Your task is to find 10 bits of information to hide in your puzzle, but you must not repeat information that you used in Step 3. DO NOT show where the words are. Fill up empty squares with random letters. Remember to keep a note of where your answers are hidden but do not show your friends. When you have a complete puzzle, exchange it with a friend to solve each other's puzzle.

Step 5

Now make up 10 questions (not "answers" this time) based on the same chapter used in the previous two tasks. Again, you must find NEW information that you have not yet used. Now it's getting hard to find that new information! Again, give your questions to a friend to answer.

Step 6

As you have been doing the puzzles, your brain has been actively searching for new information. Now write a NEW LIST that contains only the new information you have discovered when doing the puzzles. Your new list is the one to look at repeatedly for short bursts over the next few days. Try to remember more and more of it without looking at it. After a few days, you should be able to add words from your second list to your first list as you increase the information in your long-term memory.

FINALLY! Be inspired...

Make a list of different revision ideas and beside each one write **THINGS I HAVE** tried, **THINGS I WILL** try and **THINGS I MIGHT** try. Don't be scared of trying something new.

And remember – "FAIL TO PREPARE AND PREPARE TO FAIL!"

Higher Modern Studies

The Exam

There are two papers in the Higher Modern Studies exam. Paper 1 lasts 90 minutes and consists of four essays of 15 marks each, so there are a total of 60 marks available.

Paper 2 lasts 1 hour and 15 minutes and consists of four short evaluation questions worth a total of 10 marks and a report or Decision Making Exercise worth 20 marks. There are a total of 30 marks available for this paper.

Structure of Paper 1

In Paper 1, you must complete four essay questions, each of which are worth 15 marks:

- One from Section A – Political Issues in the UK
- One from Section B – Social Issues in the UK
- One from Section C – International Issues

Plus:

- One other from either Section A or Section C

You should remember that there is only one question per Study Theme except within Section B (Social Issues – Health and Wealth Inequalities in the UK) where one question should be completed from a choice of two. You may complete your four essays in the order that best suits you.

Types of question

Questions in Paper 1 are analytical in style. Analysis questions start:

- Assess...
- Critically examine the view...
- To what extent...
- "Statement." Discuss...

To answer a question you will have to show knowledge and understanding of an issue, but also be able to analyse, evaluate and comment on the arguments surrounding a given issue.

Common candidate errors

Each year, the most common candidate errors in the Higher Modern Studies exam are:

Paper 2 is the report or DME. Candidates must answer four short source-based questions before writing a report. The report is based on the UK Social Issues study theme.

Paper 1

1. Failure to answer the question asked
2. Poor time management or the completion of only three essays
3. Poor essay structure or lack of development / explanation

4. Poor, outdated and inaccurate exemplification
5. Lack of balanced comment (description as opposed to analysis)
6. Failure to provide insightful conclusions

Paper 2

1. Poor structure
2. Failure to make full use of Sources A and B and all the Statistical Sources (C1–C5)
3. Poor synthesis of arguments to support a recommendation or when identifying / commenting on opposing arguments
4. Failure to include accurate, relevant and up-to-date background knowledge

The road to success

In recent years examiners have commented positively on many of the responses they have encountered. Most schools prepare their candidates thoroughly and an increasing number of students are achieving top marks. There are few weak candidates or schools. However, evidence from past examinations would suggest that a greater number of candidates would attain higher grades if they improved their essay or report/DME writing technique, as opposed to, for example, attempting to write "all they know about an issue" in an answer.

The information below is an attempt to address the common errors above and to provide some hints and tips to help you out!

Paper 1 – Some hints and tips

Points to remember when answering questions in Paper 1:

1. Answer the question asked. Take time to consider the question before starting. If the question refers to social class as a factor influencing voting behaviour then make this the focus of the answer. However, the question may also ask about the importance of social class as a factor influencing voting behaviour. To pass, your answer must also provide evaluative comment, i.e. comment on the importance of social class as a factor affecting voting behaviour.

2. Tackling four questions in 90 minutes divides as only 22.5 minutes per question, so be sure to practise essay questions under timed conditions without notes, books, etc. This is invaluable preparation for the final exam.

3. Make sure that you structure your essay and offer development and explanation where required. For example, in response to a question which asks, "To what extent does social class affect voting behaviour?" One possible structure is:

P Point   Social class continues to affect the way in which around 40% of the electorate vote.

E Explain   Wealthier people (Social class A/B) more often voted Conservative in the 2010 UK General Election.

E Example   According to MORI, the Conservatives attracted support from 39% of all AB voters in the 2010 UK General Election.

A good structure ensures a response develops a line of argument, provides for better synthesis and encourages exemplification.

4. Avoid outdated and inaccurate examples. Quality exemplification is highly creditworthy so include up-to-date examples wherever possible.

5. Provide balanced comment (description and analysis). To pass (8 or more out of 15) a Higher Modern Studies essay must provide both Knowledge (description / explanation / exemplification) and analysis (evaluation or balanced comment). For point 3 (above) the example only provides knowledge. Therefore, comment that provides analysis is required. For example:

P Point   Social class continues to influence the way around 40% of the electorate vote.

E Explain   Wealthier people (Social class A/B) more often voted Conservative in the 2010 General Election. This is partly explained by the Conservatives traditional support for lower taxation.

E Example   According to MORI, the Conservatives attracted support from 39% of all AB voters in the 2010 UK General Election.

B Balance   However, there were many AB voters who voted for other parties, e.g. Labour polled 29% of the AB voters in 2010.

"Balance" words include "however", "but" and "on the other hand". Balance does not require you to provide an equal number of reasons for or against an issue. It means clarifying your points to extend understanding and increase accuracy.

6. Within an essay, aim to make relevant conclusions. For example, if the question asks, "To what extent…", then your response should provide an overall understanding of the extent of the factor in question.

Paper 2 – Some hints and tips

Evaluating questions

You should answer evaluating questions (Q1-4) **only** using the sources provided. The evaluating questions run in the same order as the paper, i.e. question 1 relates to information in the first half of source A, question 2 relates to information in the second half of source A, etc.

You should always "quote" fully from sources A or B before explaining why your selected statement is exaggerated or the extent to which it is accurate.

The headings of the statistical sources (C1–C5) should help you locate the correct statement to quote. When you encounter the phrase "To what extent", it means that in Higher Modern Studies the view is partly correct and partly incorrect.

You should try to keep your answers to these questions brief. Quote only the view and the explanation for your answer in relation to the information in the source.

The DME or report

1. When it comes to structuring your report/DME, remember that it is not an extended essay. You should try to write in the style of a report, i.e. with sub-headings, an introduction, arguments to support your recommendation, arguments to oppose a recommendation, a conclusion and references (in line or in the margin).

2. Sources A and B will contain several arguments for or against a decision, so make good use of these sources, and all of the statistical sources from C1–C5. Aim to use each of the statistical sources at least once.

3. High marks are awarded for reports and DMEs that synthesise the main argument from sources A and B with the statistical sources and background knowledge. Remember that the written sources (A+B) will be partly biased. Think carefully when using these sources.

4. Sources A and B contain "coat hangers" designed to invite background knowledge. For example, "other benefits" – give names of state benefit, e.g. Universal Credit; "individualist approach" – explain individualist approach to welfare, etc. or develop specialist terminology such as "dependency culture".

Good luck!

Remember that the rewards for passing Higher Modern Studies are well worth it! Your pass will help you get the future you want for yourself. In the exam, be confident in your own ability. If you're not sure how to answer a question, trust your instincts and just give it a go anyway – keep calm and don't panic! GOOD LUCK!

[BLANK PAGE]

X236/301

NATIONAL
QUALIFICATIONS
2010

TUESDAY, 25 MAY
9.00 AM – 10.30 AM

MODERN STUDIES
HIGHER
Paper 1

Candidates should answer **FOUR** questions:

- **ONE** from Section A

and

- **ONE** from Section B

and

- **ONE** from Section C

and

ONE OTHER from **EITHER** Section A **OR** Section C

Section A: Political Issues in the United Kingdom

Section B: Social Issues in the United Kingdom

Section C: International Issues.

Each question is worth 15 marks.

SECTION A—Political Issues in the United Kingdom
Each question is worth 15 marks

STUDY THEME 1A: DEVOLVED DECISION MAKING IN SCOTLAND

Question A1

With devolution there is no need for Scottish representation at Westminster.
Discuss.

STUDY THEME 1B: DECISION MAKING IN CENTRAL GOVERNMENT

Question A2

Critically examine the view that the UK Parliament has little control over the Executive.

STUDY THEME 1C: POLITICAL PARTIES AND THEIR POLICIES
(INCLUDING THE SCOTTISH DIMENSION)

Question A3

To what extent do party members decide their party's policies?

STUDY THEME 1D: ELECTORAL SYSTEMS, VOTING AND POLITICAL
ATTITUDES

Question A4

The Single Transferable Vote electoral system provides for better representation than First Past the Post.
Discuss.

SECTION B — Social Issues in the United Kingdom

Each question is worth 15 marks

STUDY THEME 2: WEALTH AND HEALTH INEQUALITIES IN THE UNITED KINGDOM

EITHER

Question B5

Individual lifestyle choices limit good health more than any other factor.

Discuss.

OR

Question B6

To what extent have government policies reduced gender **and/or** ethnic inequalities?

[Turn over for Section C on *Page four*

SECTION C — International Issues

Each question is worth 15 marks

STUDY THEME 3A: THE REPUBLIC OF SOUTH AFRICA

Question C7

To what extent is South Africa a multi–party democracy?

STUDY THEME 3B: THE PEOPLE'S REPUBLIC OF CHINA

Question C8

Critically examine the view that there is little opposition to the Communist Party in China.

STUDY THEME 3C: THE UNITED STATES OF AMERICA

Question C9

Assess the impact of recent immigration on the USA.

STUDY THEME 3D: THE EUROPEAN UNION

Question C10

Critically examine the view that the Common Agricultural and Fisheries Policies have benefited the member states of the European Union.

STUDY THEME 3E: THE POLITICS OF DEVELOPMENT IN AFRICA

Question C11

With reference to specific African countries (excluding the Republic of South Africa):

The United Nations Organisation (UNO) has been effective in promoting development. Discuss.

STUDY THEME 3F: GLOBAL SECURITY

Question C12

Assess the effectiveness of NATO in achieving international peace and security.

[END OF QUESTION PAPER]

X236/302

NATIONAL QUALIFICATIONS 2010	TUESDAY, 25 MAY 10.50 AM – 12.05 PM	MODERN STUDIES HIGHER Paper 2

Summary of Decision Making Exercise

You are a health policy adviser. You have been asked to prepare a report for the Scottish Government Cabinet Secretary for Health and Wellbeing in which you recommend or reject a proposal to introduce Well Man Clinics to every part of Scotland.

Before beginning the task, you must answer a number of evaluating questions (Questions 1–3) based on the source material provided. The source material is:

SOURCE A: Well Man Clinics are an Urgent Priority

SOURCE B: Well Man Clinics are a Waste of Resources

SOURCE C: Statistical Information

SOURCE A: WELL MAN CLINICS ARE AN URGENT PRIORITY

Numerous reports prove that the health of men in this country is worse than the health of women. Urgent Government action to close the gender health gap is required. Year after year, male death rates are higher than female death rates for all causes and men have lower life expectancy across Scotland. While attention has, in the past, been focused on improving
5 women's health, recent equality legislation now demands that all groups receive equal access to health advice and health care services. Therefore, one immediate and practical response to reduce the gender health gap must be to expand the number of Well Man Clinics to every part of Scotland.

Well Man Clinics are appointment-free, drop-in facilities where men can choose to receive
10 expert health advice on a range of health matters such as diet and fitness or on those issues particular only to males. Any man voluntarily attending would have the opportunity to speak to a dedicated health professional and the advice offered would be given in a supportive and non-judgemental way. In some parts of Scotland, Well Man Clinics have already been piloted. So far these appear to have worked well. Initial reviews show that the opening of
15 Well Man Clinics has been welcomed by men. Establishing Well Man Clinics in the rest of Scotland would have a significant impact on reducing male ill-health. For a relatively small NHS investment there would be enormous long-term financial savings. Prevention is always better than cure.

Well Man Clinics would work alongside the many educational health campaigns already being
20 run by the Scottish Government. These clinics will offer men positive choices in life. This is not a case of government lecturing men to live healthier lives. As things stand, there is a need to encourage men to consider their own health. Men are not making full use of traditional GP services. Health studies indicate that most men want to live healthier lifestyles but they need advice and support within their communities to enable this to happen. Studies show
25 that too many men are making the wrong lifestyle choices. They continue to smoke, they fail to take enough exercise or they eat a poor diet. Recent figures on alcohol consumption make uncomfortable reading. Annually, the number of males exceeding the recommended alcohol intake guidelines continues to increase.

Everyone knows there is no "quick fix" to improving men's health. Well Man Clinics would
30 be just one part of a wider approach to health care that looks at tackling the various causes of Scotland's poor health. However, targeted intervention at the men who are most at risk does work. Well Man Clinics should be set up in all areas of Scotland.

Karen MacDonald, University Lecturer

SOURCE B: WELL MAN CLINICS ARE A WASTE OF RESOURCES

Expanding the number of Well Man Clinics is not the correct approach to tackling Scotland's poor health record. Well Man Clinics will make no impact on those men who most need to change their lifestyles. The "nanny state" approach will make little or no impact on the group of men putting themselves at the greatest risk. Instead, it is the "worried well" who
5 will attend. Well Man Clinics will be used, in the main, by health-conscious, middle class professionals who already lead healthy lifestyles. There can be very few men who do not already know that smoking, alcohol, a lack of exercise or poor diet are bad for their health. In any event, more women now smoke than men in every age group. An increase in the number of male-only clinics targeting men's health will do nothing to reduce gender health inequality.

10 Instead of wasting scarce NHS resources on expanding the number of Well Man Clinics, the Scottish Government needs to address the underlying causes of social and economic inequality. For example, the link between poverty and poor health has been well documented. Priority must be given to policies that reduce poverty and not those that deal exclusively with male ill-health. There are already plenty of support agencies available to help those men who
15 wish to lead healthier lifestyles. Resources allocated to expanding Well Man Clinics can only mean a reduction in services elsewhere in the NHS.

Well Man Clinics are well intentioned but they do not work. One evaluation of the pilot projects suggests that "one size does not fit all". Not all men want separate daytime health services for males. Surveys show most men wanted Well Man Clinics open in the evenings and
20 a majority were unhappy with the information they received. Instead a variety of approaches to changing men's attitudes to their health is required. The previous Scottish Government spent £4 million on Well Man Clinics yet the success of these clinics has been, at best, mixed. This is in stark contrast to other health education programmes, such as those dealing with the use of illegal drugs, which have been far more successful. At a time when there are many
25 competing demands on the NHS budget, £4 million does not represent best value in the use of taxpayers' money.

Tackling the health inequalities that exist in Scotland today requires something greater than what is offered by Well Man Clinics. In other countries where health inequalities have been successfully reduced a collectivist approach has been adopted. The Scottish Government,
30 and the UK Government, have introduced some imaginative policies to improve health for all. Unfortunately, Well Man Clinics is not one of them.

William Walker, Anti-Poverty Campaigner

[Turn over for Source C on *Pages four, five* and *six*

SOURCE C: STATISTICAL INFORMATION

SOURCE C1 (*a*)   Male and female death rates by selected causes in Scotland, 2003–2007 (per 100 000 population)

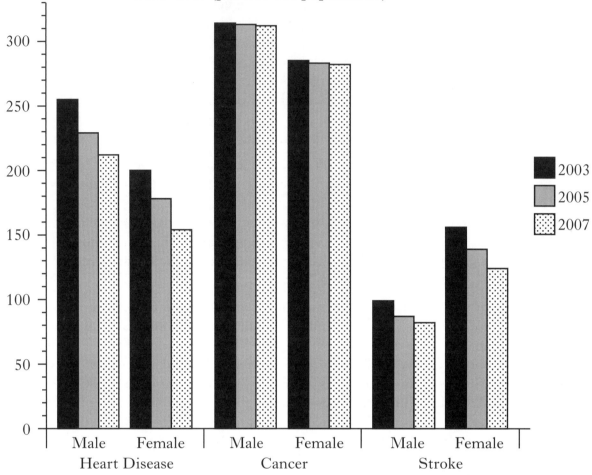

SOURCE C1 (*b*)   Male and female life expectancy at birth in Scotland, 2005 (by selected council area)

	Male	*Female*
Aberdeen City	75·0	79·9
Dundee City	73·0	78·4
East Ayrshire	73·7	78·0
East Renfrewshire	76·8	81·0
Glasgow City	69·9	76·7
Highland	75·0	80·3
Inverclyde	71·1	77·9
Perth and Kinross	76·4	80·6
Scottish Borders	75·8	80·0
West Dunbartonshire	71·0	77·5
All Scotland	**74·2**	**79·2**

Both Sources: Adapted from General Register Office for Scotland data

SOURCE C: (continued)

SOURCE C2 (*a*)   Percentage of Scottish adults exceeding recommended guidelines on alcohol intake: 1999–2005

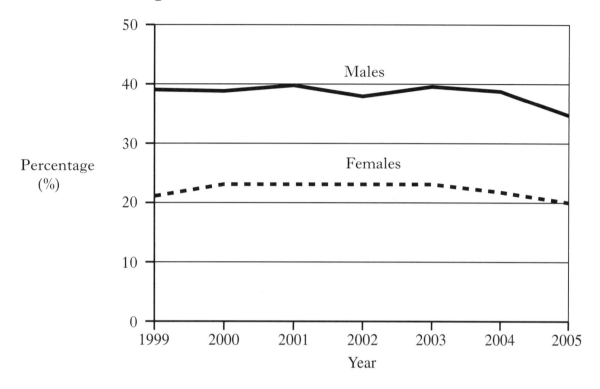

SOURCE C2 (*b*)   Percentage of Scottish adults who smoke; by age and sex (2005)

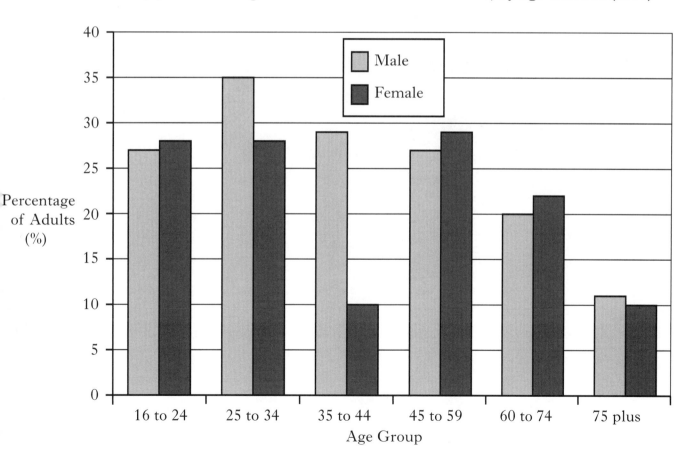

Both Sources: Adapted from Scottish Government data

SOURCE C: **(continued)**

SOURCE C3   **SURVEY OF THE ATTITUDES OF MEN ATTENDING SOME OF THE WELL MAN CLINICS PILOT PROJECTS**

SOURCE C3 (*a*)   **Were you happy with the information you received at the Well Man Clinics?**

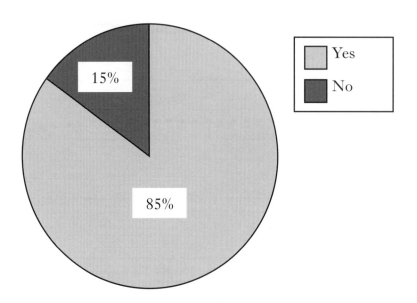

SOURCE C3 (*b*)   **Would you have liked to have seen Well Man Clinics open in the evenings?**

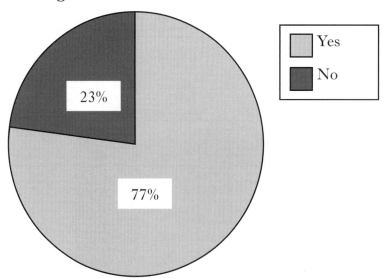

Source: East Glasgow Well Man Clinics Final Evaluation Report, September 2006

Marks

DECISION MAKING EXERCISE

QUESTIONS

Questions 1 to 3 are based on Sources A to C on Pages 2–6. Answer Questions 1 to 3 before attempting Question 4.

In Questions 1 to 3, use <u>only</u> the Sources described in each question.

Question 1

Use **only** *Source C1(a), Source C1(b) and Source A.*

To what extent does the evidence support Karen MacDonald?   **3**

Question 2

(*a*)   *Use* **only** *Source C2(a) and Source A.*

Why might Karen MacDonald be accused of exaggeration?   **2**

(*b*)   *Use* **only** *Source C2(b) and Source B.*

Why might William Walker be accused of exaggeration?   **2**

Question 3

Use **only** *Source C3(a), Source C3(b) and Source B.*

To what extent does the evidence support William Walker?   **3**

(10)

Marks

Question 4

DECISION MAKING TASK

You are a health policy adviser. You have been asked to prepare a report for the Scottish Government Cabinet Secretary for Health and Wellbeing in which you recommend or reject a proposal to introduce Well Man Clinics to every part of Scotland.

Your answer should be written in the style of a *report*.

Your report should:

- recommend or reject the proposal to introduce Well Man Clinics to every part of Scotland

- provide arguments to support your recommendation

- identify and comment on any arguments which may be presented by those who oppose your recommendation

- refer to all Sources provided

  AND

- **must** include relevant background knowledge.

The written and statistical sources which are provided are:

SOURCE A: Well Man Clinics are an Urgent Priority

SOURCE B: Well Man Clinics are a Waste of Resources

SOURCE C: Statistical Information

(20)

Total: 30 Marks

[END OF QUESTION PAPER]

[BLANK PAGE]

X236/301

NATIONAL
QUALIFICATIONS
2011

TUESDAY, 31 MAY
9.00 AM – 10.30 AM

MODERN STUDIES
HIGHER
Paper 1

Candidates should answer **FOUR** questions:

*   **ONE** from Section A

and

*   **ONE** from Section B

and

*   **ONE** from Section C

and

ONE OTHER from **EITHER** Section A **OR** Section C

Section A: Political Issues in the United Kingdom

Section B: Social Issues in the United Kingdom

Section C: International Issues.

Each question is worth 15 marks.

SECTION A—Political Issues in the United Kingdom
Each question is worth 15 marks

STUDY THEME 1A: DEVOLVED DECISION MAKING IN SCOTLAND

Question A1

To what extent do Members of the Scottish Parliament (MSPs) influence decision making in the Scottish Government?

STUDY THEME 1B: DECISION MAKING IN CENTRAL GOVERNMENT

Question A2

Some groups outside Parliament have more influence on decision making in Central Government than others.

Discuss.

STUDY THEME 1C: POLITICAL PARTIES AND THEIR POLICIES (INCLUDING THE SCOTTISH DIMENSION)

Question A3

Political parties elect their leaders differently but the choice of leader is crucial to electoral success.

Discuss.

STUDY THEME 1D: ELECTORAL SYSTEMS, VOTING AND POLITICAL ATTITUDES

Question A4

Some factors affecting voting behaviour are more important than others.
Discuss.

SECTION B — Social Issues in the United Kingdom

Each question is worth 15 marks

STUDY THEME 2: WEALTH AND HEALTH INEQUALITIES IN THE UNITED KINGDOM

EITHER

Question B5

Poverty is the most important factor that affects health.

Discuss.

OR

Question B6

Health and welfare provision should be the responsibility of government.

Discuss.

[Turn over for Section C on *Page four*

SECTION C — International Issues

Each question is worth 15 marks

STUDY THEME 3A: THE REPUBLIC OF SOUTH AFRICA

Question C7

Assess the effectiveness of government policies to reduce social and economic inequalities in South Africa.

STUDY THEME 3B: THE PEOPLE'S REPUBLIC OF CHINA

Question C8

To what extent has social and economic change benefited the people of China?

STUDY THEME 3C: THE UNITED STATES OF AMERICA

Question C9

Assess the effectiveness of government policies to reduce social and economic inequalities in the USA.

STUDY THEME 3D: THE EUROPEAN UNION

Question C10

There is little disagreement within the EU over social and economic policies.

Discuss.

STUDY THEME 3E: THE POLITICS OF DEVELOPMENT IN AFRICA

Question C11

With reference to specific African countries (excluding the Republic of South Africa):

Education and health care are the most important factors in achieving successful development in Africa.

Discuss.

STUDY THEME 3F: GLOBAL SECURITY

Question C12

The UN must reform to be more effective when dealing with threats to international peace and security.

Discuss.

[END OF QUESTION PAPER]

X236/302

| NATIONAL QUALIFICATIONS 2011 | TUESDAY, 31 MAY 10.50 AM – 12.05 PM | MODERN STUDIES HIGHER Paper 2 |

Summary of Decision Making Exercise

You are an independent policy researcher. You have been asked to prepare a report for the Low Pay Commission in which you recommend or reject a proposal to increase the value of the UK's National Minimum Wage (NMW) to £8 per hour for adult workers.

Before beginning the task, you must answer a number of evaluating questions (Questions 1–4) based on the source material provided. The source material is:

SOURCE A: A Living Wage of £8 per hour

SOURCE B: Unwelcome and Unaffordable

SOURCE C: Statistical Information

SOURCE A: A LIVING WAGE OF £8 PER HOUR

When introduced, the National Minimum Wage (NMW) was intended to end poverty wages for millions of low paid workers. Updated annually on the recommendation of the Low Pay Commission, the NMW sets a minimum hourly payment to which all workers are entitled. However, since 2007, the number of people on low incomes has risen while
5 the relative value of the NMW in the UK is one of the lowest in the developed world. Therefore, if Government is serious in its attempts to meet its own targets to reduce poverty in this country, the NMW for adult workers should be increased to £8 per hour.

Lifting people out of poverty through work is widely seen as the best way to tackle
10 inequality in society. Those who favour a collectivist approach understand the value of a more equal society. In recent years, the extent to which society has become more divided has become all too clear. There is a wealth of evidence that shows poverty, and the social problems poverty creates, is increasing. Tinkering with the tax and benefits system has not reduced the levels of poverty in this country. Radical change is required.

15 There will be many benefits arising from increasing the adult NMW to £8 per hour. To begin with, the embarrassing, complicated and costly process of means-tested benefits could be scrapped. An £8 per hour NMW is simple, straightforward, dignified and makes work pay. It would mean an end to employers paying poverty wages with the State making up the difference between low wages and what is needed to avoid hardship.
20 Each low paid worker will immediately receive an increase in income. Jobs that were previously hard to fill because of low pay will become more attractive. In time, employers will benefit from a more stable, better rewarded and better committed workforce. Demand for goods will rise, leading to higher employment levels. In the years to come, Government will benefit through increased tax returns and reduced
25 Social Security payments. Few people believe that an £8 per hour NMW will push up wage rates in other areas of employment. An £8 NMW is a "win-win" scenario.

To those who oppose £8 per hour NMW I say this: the UK cannot compete with the emerging nations of China, India and Brazil when it comes to low skilled manufacturing jobs. If our economy is to grow, the country must look to develop a highly skilled,
30 highly rewarded workforce. The current NMW does not encourage unemployed people to move into paid employment. Many politicians believe that the NMW is too low. Introducing an £8 per hour NMW will energise our workforce and bring an end to poverty wages once and for all.

Ken Dorward, Anti-poverty Campaigner

SOURCE B: **UNWELCOME AND UNAFFORDABLE**

Demands to increase the adult National Minimum Wage (NMW) to £8 per hour must be resisted by the Low Pay Commission. At a time when the UK economy is only slowly recovering from the worst recession in fifty years, it would be economic madness to burden employers with extra wage costs. Every year since its introduction there has
5 been a rise in the annual percentage rate of the NMW. In some years, the annual percentage rise in the NMW has been greater than the annual percentage rise in average earnings. The UK now has very few households living in poverty compared to other European Union countries. The rates of pay for the NMW currently ensure there are no poverty wages in this country. An £8 adult NMW is simply not needed.

10 There is a second reason why an £8 per hour adult NMW must be resisted. It is not the responsibility of government to reduce poverty—it is up to the individual to work harder, be better educated and become more skilled. Only when individuals strive to improve themselves can people be permanently lifted out of poverty. All too often people of working age in this country expect the State to provide for them. There is
15 already a huge range of benefits to support the poorest groups in society. The UK's "dependency culture" must come to an end.

People work hard to ensure the success of their businesses. In the modern economy, wage levels reflect the value placed on different workers by society. Why should workers with the least skills and fewest qualifications be paid more than they are worth? Opinion
20 surveys show that the public agree with the idea of an NMW but an £8 NMW would have a disastrous effect on businesses such as hotels and restaurants where the majority of low paid workers are found. In a world where multinational companies move from country to country seeking ever cheaper wage rates, our foreign competitors will hardly be able to believe their luck. In a number of countries in Europe, such as Denmark and
25 Italy, there is no NMW and for good reason: it is unwelcome and unaffordable.

Supporters of an £8 adult NMW must consider the knock-on effect of their proposal. If wages for the lowest paid are increased, other workers will demand higher wages. Employers will be faced with rising wage demands that they simply cannot afford. To meet the cost of an £8 adult NMW employers will have to lay off staff at a time when
30 UK unemployment rates are historically high. Trade union industrial action will be sure to follow. It is clear that those groups demanding an £8 adult NMW have not considered fully the consequences of their proposal.

Christine Kelly, Businessperson

[Turn over for Source C on *Pages four, five* and *six*

SOURCE C: STATISTICAL INFORMATION

SOURCE C1   Numbers of people in the UK on low incomes in millions 1979–2009

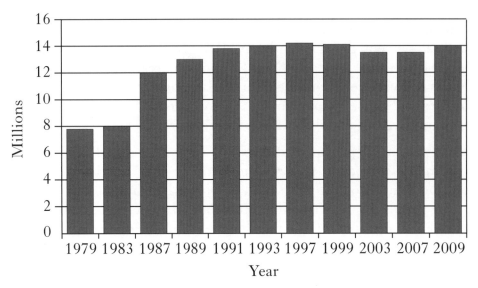

Source: Adapted from the Poverty Site

SOURCE C2   Comparison of the relative value of the national minimum wage in Pounds (£s) between selected developed countries, 2008

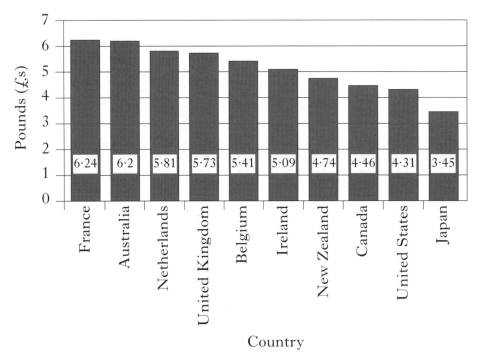

Country

*The bar graph gives the value of the adult hourly NMW in selected countries if paid in UK Pounds (£s)

Source: Adapted from Low Pay Commission Report 2009

SOURCE C: (CONTINUED)

SOURCE C3 Public opinion survey on the National Minimum Wage 2009

(i)   Do you agree with the idea of a National Minimum Wage (NMW)?

Yes 85%   No 10%   Don't know 5%

(ii)   Do you think that the current NMW is . . .

Too high?   15%   Too low?   35%
About right?   40%   Don't know.   10%

(iii) Do you think a higher NMW would harm the UK economy?

Yes 50%   No 35%   Don't know 15%

(iv)   Do you think a higher NMW will push up wages in other areas of employment?

Yes 40%   No 35%   Don't know 25%

Source: UK telephone survey, 1004 people, August 2009 (adapted)

SOURCE C4 Percentage (%) of households in poverty in selected EU countries 2009

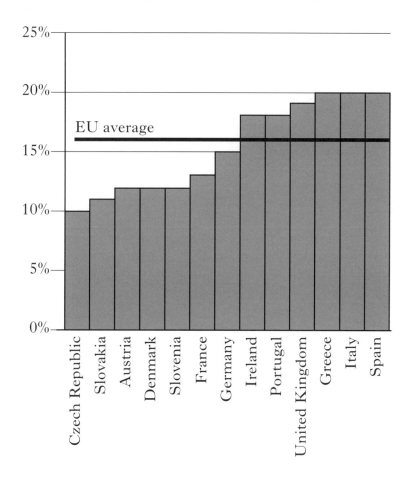

Source: Adapted from Eurostat; updated Jan 2009

SOURCE C: (CONTINUED)

SOURCE C5   Types of employment where low paid workers were found [in percentages (%) in 2009]

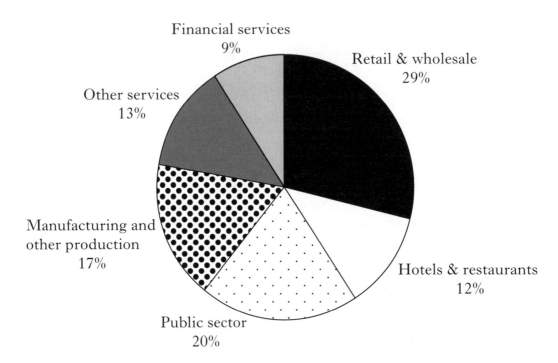

Source: Adapted from Labour Force Survey; updated March 2009

DECISION MAKING EXERCISE

QUESTIONS

Marks

Questions 1 to 4 are based on Sources A to C on pages 2–6. Answer Questions 1 to 4 before attempting Question 5.

In Questions 1 to 4, use <u>only</u> the Sources described in each question.

Question 1

*Use **only** Source C1, C2 and Source A.*

To what extent does the evidence support Ken Dorward?

3

Question 2

*Use **only** Source C3 and Source A.*

Why might Ken Dorward be accused of exaggeration?

2

Question 3

*Use **only** Source C4 and Source B.*

Why might Christine Kelly be accused of exaggeration?

2

Question 4

*Use **only** Source C3, C5 and Source B.*

To what extent does the evidence support Christine Kelly?

3

(10)

Marks

Question 5

DECISION MAKING TASK

You are an independent policy researcher. You have been asked to prepare a report for the Low Pay Commission in which you recommend or reject a proposal to increase the value of the UK's National Minimum Wage (NMW) to £8 per hour for adult workers.

Your answer should be written in the style of a *report*.

Your report should:

- recommend or reject the proposal to increase the UK's National Minimum Wage (NMW) to £8 per hour for adult workers

- provide arguments to support your recommendation

- identify and comment on any arguments which may be presented by those who oppose your recommendation

- refer to all the Sources provided

  AND

- **must** include relevant background knowledge.

The written and statistical sources which are provided are:

SOURCE A: A Living Wage of £8 per hour

SOURCE B: Unwelcome and Unaffordable

SOURCE C: Statistical Information

(20)

Total: 30 Marks

[END OF QUESTION PAPER]

HODDER
GIBSON
LEARN MORE

[BLANK PAGE]

X236/12/01

NATIONAL
QUALIFICATIONS
2012

FRIDAY, 11 MAY
9.00 AM – 10.30 AM

MODERN STUDIES
HIGHER
Paper 1

Candidates should answer **FOUR** questions:

• **ONE** from Section A

and

• **ONE** from Section B

and

• **ONE** from Section C

and

ONE OTHER from **EITHER** Section A **OR** Section C

Section A: Political Issues in the United Kingdom

Section B: Social Issues in the United Kingdom

Section C: International Issues.

Each question is worth 15 marks.

SECTION A—Political Issues in the United Kingdom
Each question is worth 15 marks

STUDY THEME 1A: DEVOLVED DECISION MAKING IN SCOTLAND

Question A1

In carrying out its functions, local government in Scotland has come into conflict with the Scottish Government.

Discuss.

STUDY THEME 1B: DECISION MAKING IN CENTRAL GOVERNMENT

Question A2

To what extent is the UK Parliament effective in controlling the powers of the Prime Minister?

STUDY THEME 1C: POLITICAL PARTIES AND THEIR POLICIES (INCLUDING THE SCOTTISH DIMENSION)

Question A3

Critically examine the view that there are few policy differences between the main political parties.

STUDY THEME 1D: ELECTORAL SYSTEMS, VOTING AND POLITICAL ATTITUDES

Question A4

To what extent is the media the most important factor affecting voter behaviour?

SECTION B—Social Issues in the United Kingdom

Each question is worth 15 marks

STUDY THEME 2: WEALTH AND HEALTH INEQUALITIES IN
THE UNITED KINGDOM

EITHER

Question B5

The UK's Welfare State continues to meet its aims.

Discuss.

OR

Question B6

Critically examine the view that Government has failed to reduce gender **or** race inequalities in the UK.

[Turn over for Section C on *Page four*

SECTION C—International Issues
Each question is worth 15 marks

STUDY THEME 3A: THE REPUBLIC OF SOUTH AFRICA

Question C7

The political strength of the African National Congress does not threaten democracy in South Africa.

Discuss.

STUDY THEME 3B: THE PEOPLE'S REPUBLIC OF CHINA

Question C8

In China, democracy has been extended and human rights improved.

Discuss.

STUDY THEME 3C: THE UNITED STATES OF AMERICA

Question C9

To what extent does Congress act as an effective check on the powers of the President?

STUDY THEME 3D: THE EUROPEAN UNION

Question C10

Assess the importance of the European Parliament in decision making within the European Union (EU).

STUDY THEME 3E: THE POLITICS OF DEVELOPMENT IN AFRICA

Question C11

With reference to specific African countries (excluding the Republic of South Africa):

Assess the effectiveness of foreign aid in promoting development.

STUDY THEME 3F: GLOBAL SECURITY

Question C12

International terrorism is seen by NATO as the main threat to global peace and security.

Discuss.

[END OF QUESTION PAPER]

X236/12/02

NATIONAL
QUALIFICATIONS
2012

FRIDAY, 11 MAY
10.50 AM – 12.05 PM

MODERN STUDIES
HIGHER
Paper 2

Summary of Decision Making Exercise

You are an education policy adviser. You have been asked to prepare a report for the Scottish Government Cabinet Secretary for Education and Life Long Learning in which you recommend or reject *Breakthrough*, a proposal to set aside at least 33% of places at Scottish universities for young people from a working-class background.

Before beginning the DME (Q5), you must answer a number of evaluating questions (Q1–4) based on the source material provided. The source material is:

SOURCE A: Genuine Educational Equality

SOURCE B: One Inequality Replaces Another

SOURCE C: Statistical Information

SOURCE A: GENUINE EDUCATIONAL EQUALITY

In order to achieve the highest paid employment, a degree from university is normally required. Equality of access to university is an important part of a progressive society. However, in Scotland there is little equality of educational opportunity. Statistics show Scottish universities have, on average, a minority of students with parents from a

5 working-class background, with Edinburgh and Glasgow universities having the lowest figures. In other European countries, legislation has increased the number of students from working-class backgrounds going to university. In the interests of fairness and to improve social mobility, Scotland needs to follow Europe's lead. Positive discrimination has worked well in other countries and would work well here.

10 *Breakthrough* is a proposal to tackle higher education inequality. It requires Scottish universities to set aside at least 33% of undergraduate places for young people from a working-class background. To maintain standards, only those who achieve the entry requirements for the course for which they apply will gain entry to university. Many young people whose parents may not have had the opportunity to benefit from a

15 university education, can now focus on their studies with an expectation that a university place is theirs, if they attain the relevant qualifications.

There will be many educational advantages if the *Breakthrough* proposal is adopted. Higher education exam results would improve as evidence suggests that students from working-class backgrounds often attain better university qualifications in the

20 long-term than their middle-class peers. University life would be enriched by having a student intake that is socially more diverse. Secondary schools already provide many programmes that encourage young people to pursue a university education but more needs to be done. *Breakthrough* is that next step.

Breakthrough is also important to the future of the Scottish economy. It will help to

25 ensure that more of our talented young people achieve their educational potential. Employers will gain as the quality of graduate improves. The public services will benefit from the next generation of senior judges, lawyers and health professionals having wider life experience. Currently, the professions are completely dominated by those who have been privately educated at fee-paying schools. How can this be fair in

30 the 21st Century? Given time, *Breakthrough* will sit alongside other government policies that have been successful in improving educational opportunity.

Finally, government, not individuals, is best placed to reduce inequality in society. There is a great deal of evidence to prove that legislation to reduce different types of social inequalities works. The law has helped improve the position of women. Many

35 other disadvantaged groups have also benefited from forward-looking government action. *Breakthrough* will give hope to those less affluent groups who have been subject to a wide range of inequalities for far too long.

Stephen Morris, Scottish Education Policy Adviser

SOURCE B: ONE INEQUALITY REPLACES ANOTHER

Most initiatives that encourage young people from working-class backgrounds into higher education are to be commended. However, the *Breakthrough* proposal is a step in the wrong direction. Although *Breakthrough* retains minimum qualifications for university entrance, the reality is that many university courses are oversubscribed. If
5 33% of university places are reserved for those from working-class backgrounds, that means fewer places for other students, many of whom will be high achievers. It cannot be fair that better off university candidates are discriminated against because of their social class. The Government should not introduce a "quick fix" solution that simply replaces one inequality with another.

10 There is already a wide range of support at school and in the community to help those from disadvantaged backgrounds. Research shows that a majority of young people believe better advice and information would be most likely to help them enter a professional career. Recent Government legislation places a very high importance on equality of opportunity. In other countries, attempts to influence university intake
15 by government have been dropped and for good reason: policies such as *Breakthrough* are patronising to young people from working-class backgrounds. It effectively tells them, and future employers, that they only gained entry to university because of their background.

Breakthrough must also be rejected on economic grounds. Successful companies depend
20 on the best person for the job and not well-intentioned, but ultimately ineffective, policies such as *Breakthrough*. At the moment, businesses are going through a tough time. To compete in the global market they need the most able people emerging from university. Currently, the UK leads the world in areas such as medical science but this will end if universities cannot freely choose who they want to admit. Scotland's future
25 prosperity depends on the reputation of our great universities. We cannot dilute the quality of our graduates.

If government is serious about improving social mobility, it needs to invest more in vocational education and skills training. Today's economy requires workers who are knowledgeable, confident, responsible and able to contribute effectively. Society
30 needs to better value and reward people with these skills instead of encouraging more and more people to go to university. Many of the jobs in the future will be in the tertiary or service sector such as information technology, finance and care. Although around a third of students from working-class backgrounds study subjects such as law or biological science, it would be better to encourage young people into skilled trades
35 where wages are higher than professional salaries. Good, vocationally trained staff are in short supply. At the end of the day, it is not the Government's responsibility to engineer university intake but for individuals to work hard in order that they meet the requirements for university entrance.

Gillian Gilbert, Scottish Newspaper Columnist

[Turn over for Source C on *Pages four, five* and *six*

SOURCE C: STATISTICAL INFORMATION

SOURCE C1   Percentage (%) of students on degree courses from working-class backgrounds at selected Scottish universities 2008–09

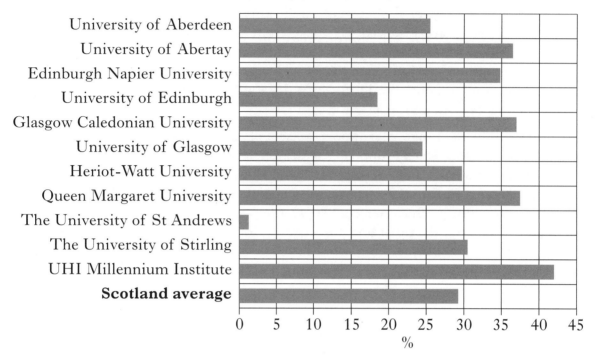

Source: Adapted from Higher Education Statistics Agency

SOURCE C2   Percentage (%) of individuals in selected professional occupations who attended fee-paying private schools

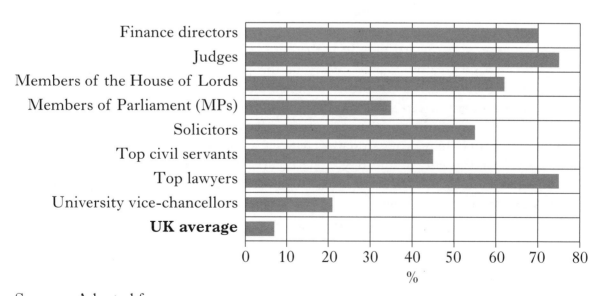

Source: Adapted from
http://www.cabinetoffice.gov.uk/media/227102/fair-access.pdf

SOURCE C: (CONTINUED)

SOURCE C3   Views of young people in percentage (%) on best way government could help them enter a professional career in percentage (%)

What do you think would be the best way to help more young people enter a professional career?				
	More financial support	Better advice and information	More work experience opportunities	Reduce discrimination
Young people	57%	22%	18%	3%

Source: Adapted from
http://www.cabinetoffice.gov.uk/media/213698/national_youth_survey.pdf

SOURCE C4   Percentage (%) of students from working-class backgrounds at UK universities by course choice (selected) 2008–09

Biological Science	33·8
Business and Administrative Studies	35·3
Computer Sciences	39·9
Education	41·4
Law	34·1
Medicine, Dentistry and Veterinary Science	18·3
Social Sciences	31·1
Subjects allied to Medicine	37·1
Average across all subjects	**32·3**

Source: Adapted from Higher Education Statistics Agency

SOURCE C: (CONTINUED)

SOURCE C5   Median* full-time earnings (£s) by occupation in Scotland, 2009

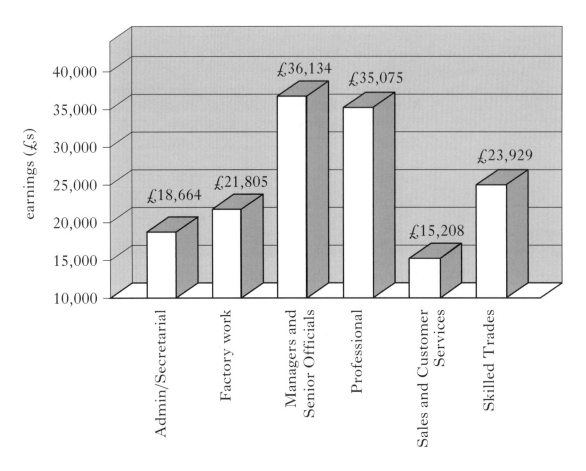

*Median—Point at which 50% of earnings are above and 50% of earnings below.

Source: http://www.scotland.gov.uk/Topics/Statistics/Browse/Labour-Market/
TrendEarnings

Marks

DECISION MAKING EXERCISE

QUESTIONS

Questions 1 to 4 are based on Sources A to C on pages 2–6. Answer Questions 1 to 4 before attempting Question 5.

In Questions 1 to 4, use <u>only</u> the Sources described in each question.

Question 1

*Use **only** Source C1 and Source A.*

To what extent does the evidence support the view of Stephen Morris?   3

Question 2

*Use **only** Source C2 and Source A.*

Why might Stephen Morris be accused of exaggeration?   2

Question 3

*Use **only** Source C3 and Source B.*

Why might Gillian Gilbert be accused of exaggeration?   2

Question 4

*Use **only** Source C4, C5 and Source B.*

To what extent does the evidence support the view of Gillian Gilbert?   3

    (10)

Marks

Question 5

DECISION MAKING EXERCISE (DME)

You are an education policy adviser. You have been asked to prepare a report for the Scottish Government Cabinet Secretary for Education and Life Long Learning in which you recommend or reject *Breakthrough*, a proposal to set aside at least 33% of places at Scottish universities for young people from a working-class background.

Your answer should be written in a style appropriate to a report.

Your report should:

- recommend or reject the proposal to set aside at least 33% of places at Scottish universities for young people from a working-class background

- provide arguments to support your decision

- identify and comment on any arguments which may be presented by those who oppose your decision

- refer to all the Sources provided

  AND

- **must** include relevant background knowledge.

The written and statistical sources which are provided are:

SOURCE A: Genuine Educational Equality

SOURCE B: One Inequality Replaces Another

SOURCE C: Statistical Information

(20)

Total: 30 marks

[END OF QUESTION PAPER]

HIGHER

2013

[BLANK PAGE]

X236/12/01

NATIONAL
QUALIFICATIONS
2013

THURSDAY, 9 MAY
9.00 AM – 10.30 AM

MODERN STUDIES
HIGHER
Paper 1

Candidates should answer **FOUR** questions:

- **ONE** from Section A

and

- **ONE** from Section B

and

- **ONE** from Section C

and

ONE OTHER from **EITHER** Section A **OR** Section C

Section A: Political Issues in the United Kingdom

Section B: Social Issues in the United Kingdom

Section C: International Issues.

Each question is worth 15 marks.

SECTION A—Political Issues in the United Kingdom
Each question is worth 15 marks

STUDY THEME 1A: DEVOLVED DECISION MAKING IN SCOTLAND

Question A1

The additional powers the Scottish Parliament has been given will allow it to better deliver "Scottish solutions to Scottish problems".

Discuss.

STUDY THEME 1B: DECISION MAKING IN CENTRAL GOVERNMENT

Question A2

Assess the importance of the Cabinet in decision making in UK Central Government.

STUDY THEME 1C: POLITICAL PARTIES AND THEIR POLICIES (INCLUDING THE SCOTTISH DIMENSION)

Question A3

To what extent do the party leaders influence their parties' policies?

STUDY THEME 1D: ELECTORAL SYSTEMS, VOTING AND POLITICAL ATTITUDES

Question A4

Critically examine the view that the Additional Member System (AMS) leads to better representation than First Past the Post (FPTP).

SECTION B—Social Issues in the United Kingdom

Each question is worth 15 marks

STUDY THEME 2: WEALTH AND HEALTH INEQUALITIES IN THE UNITED KINGDOM

EITHER

Question B5

Critically examine the view that individual lifestyle choices are the main factor preventing good health.

OR

Question B6

To what extent have government policies reduced poverty in the UK?

[Turn over for Section C on *Page four*

SECTION C—International Issues
Each question is worth 15 marks

STUDY THEME 3A: THE REPUBLIC OF SOUTH AFRICA

Question C7

To what extent have South African government policies reduced social and economic inequalities?

STUDY THEME 3B: THE PEOPLE'S REPUBLIC OF CHINA

Question C8

To what extent have Chinese government policies reduced social and economic inequalities?

STUDY THEME 3C: THE UNITED STATES OF AMERICA

Question C9

To what extent do ethnic minorities influence the outcome of elections?

STUDY THEME 3D: THE EUROPEAN UNION

Question C10

To what extent is there disagreement within the EU over social and economic issues?

STUDY THEME 3E: THE POLITICS OF DEVELOPMENT IN AFRICA

Question C11

With reference to specific African countries (excluding the Republic of South Africa):

Conflict is the main reason for a lack of development in African countries.

Discuss.

STUDY THEME 3F: GLOBAL SECURITY

Question C12

Assess the effectiveness of the UN in dealing with threats to international peace and security.

[END OF QUESTION PAPER]

X236/12/02

NATIONAL
QUALIFICATIONS
2013

THURSDAY, 9 MAY
10.50 AM – 12.05 PM

MODERN STUDIES
HIGHER
Paper 2

Summary of Decision Making Exercise

You are a health advisor to the Scottish Government. You have been asked to prepare a report in which you recommend or reject a proposal (PASS—Protection Against Second-hand Smoking) which would make it illegal to smoke directly outside entrances to buildings used by the public and in Scotland's parks and on beaches.

Before beginning the DME (Q5), you must answer a number of evaluating questions (Q1–4) based on the source material provided. The source material is:

SOURCE A: PASS will Improve Public Health

SOURCE B: Unnecessary Interference in People's Lives

SOURCE C: Statistical Information

SOURCE A: PASS WILL IMPROVE PUBLIC HEALTH

Since the Scottish Parliament passed the ban on smoking in enclosed public places, it has become commonplace for people to smoke directly outside entrances to buildings or in other public places. New legislation is needed to end this practice. The Scottish Government must support the proposal PASS (Protection Against Second-hand
5 Smoking) that will make it illegal to smoke directly outside an entrance to a public building, outdoor public places such as parks and beaches and also outside the entrances of pubs, restaurants and offices. If lighting up a cigarette in public becomes more difficult and more socially unacceptable as a result of PASS, fewer people will take up smoking and more people will have an incentive to quit. In the journey to end smoking
10 in Scottish society, PASS is the next step.

Public health campaigns are useful in persuading people to make the correct health choices but legislation restricting the availability and advertising of tobacco are also important in reducing smoking rates. The damage caused by exposure to tobacco smoke kills around 13,500 Scots each year and is responsible for around 33,500 hospital
15 admissions. Currently, Scotland has the highest daily rate of smoking in the European Union. Treating illnesses associated with smoking cost the NHS in Scotland over £400 million in 2012, funding that most Scots would rather see spent elsewhere.

Everyone should be able to enjoy the park or the beach without smoke in their faces. In many cases, non-smokers have no choice but to make their way into workplaces,
20 restaurants and bars through a group of smokers. Non-smokers who breathe in second-hand smoke take in nicotine just like smokers do. There is no safe level of exposure to second-hand smoke. In other parts of the world legislation to further restrict smoking has already proved successful. Research also suggests that the less children witness adults smoking, the less they are likely to smoke themselves.

25 Well organised smokers' rights groups will point to the rights of smokers to enjoy their habit unrestricted. They have little concern, however, for the rights of other people to breathe clean air. Further collective action is therefore required, especially in those areas most affected by poverty. Deaths linked to smoking are highest in the most deprived parts of Scotland with around half of the people in the poorest social
30 groups continuing to smoke. Extending the smoking ban will make the lives of the non-smoking majority healthier and more pleasant. It will also help smokers who need all the incentives they can get to kick an addictive, expensive and lethal habit. If we can stop parents from smoking, we can create a new smoke-free society for our young people. This is an opportunity we cannot afford to PASS up.

Carrie Brody, Anti-smoking Campaigner

SOURCE B: UNNECESSARY INTERFERENCE IN PEOPLE'S LIVES

The proposed Protecting Against Second-hand Smoking (PASS) legislation is another example of unnecessary government interference into people's lives. Currently, the answer to every minor public concern is to bring in more laws which, over time, limit people's freedoms. For any responsible government, the trivial issue of adults choosing
5 to smoke in the fresh air should be at the bottom of its list of priorities. In Scotland, smoking is no longer the public health danger it used to be and there are many more pressing social problems Scottish politicians need to tackle.

Those who choose to smoke are aware that smoking, like many other lifestyle choices, damages their health. By all means continue to educate the public, particularly the
10 young, about the dangers of smoking. Evidence suggests that those under the age of 20 are the age group most likely to smoke. However, it is wrong to extend legislation to reduce smoking where adults understand the risk but choose to continue to smoke. Individuals, not the State, should decide the way in which adults in this country live their lives. There is already a huge range of health promoting initiatives. These
15 initiatives allow responsible citizens the opportunity to make informed choices. Smoking is also one of the few pleasures some poorer people have. These people do not need further interference in their lives by out of touch middle-class politicians.

PASS would be a huge waste of scarce public resources at a time of economic hardship. Policing smokers in parks and on beaches, then dragging them through the criminal
20 justice system, will cost millions. People could have a criminal record for lighting up a cigarette! PASS, like other "nanny state" interventions, would be completely unenforceable. When it is difficult enough to control the use of illegal drugs, what chance does the Scottish Government have in controlling the thousands of Scots who choose to smoke in public places? PASS will not result in fewer people taking
25 up smoking or more smokers quitting the habit. It will only drive smokers indoors, smoking at home in the presence of their families, harming those PASS is supposedly designed to help.

The public is aware of the hypocrisy of government policy towards smoking. While it introduces new ways to reduce smoking, it collects billions of pounds in taxes from
30 smokers. Surveys show that most people do not support an extension to the ban on smoking in public places but instead think year-on-year price rises are the best way to reduce smoking. Scotland has many more serious social and economic challenges. The Scottish Government would do better to tackle the causes of poor health, such as poverty, than harassing law-abiding citizens with a patronising, unnecessary and
35 unenforceable law.

Nick Matheson, Spokesperson for Pro-smoking Pressure Group

[Turn over for Source C on *Pages four, five* and *six*

SOURCE C: STATISTICAL INFORMATION

SOURCE C1   Percentage (%) Daily Smoking Rates in Selected EU countries (2009)

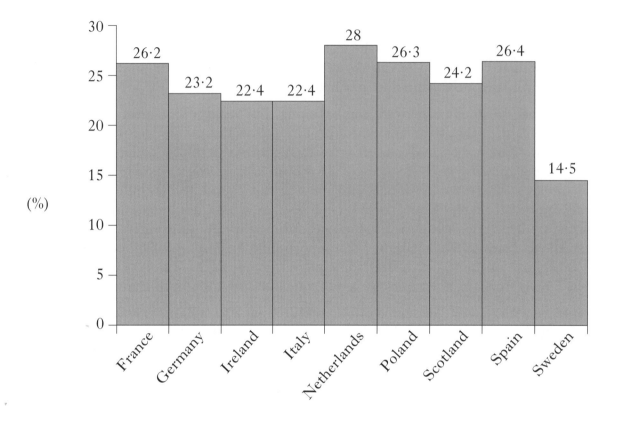

Source: WHO, Health in the European Union, 2009

SOURCE C2   Population Statistics for Low Income and Health, Selected NHS Boards in Scotland (2010)

NHS Health Board	Percentage (%) of population income deprived	Percentage (%) of deaths linked to smoking	Average male life expectancy (years)
Ayrshire and Arran	17·6	23·4	74·2
Dumfries and Galloway	14·3	19·9	76·1
Grampian	9·5	19·6	76·1
Greater Glasgow and Clyde	20·3	30·6	72·1
Orkney	10·2	11·1	75·7
Lanarkshire	16·7	22·8	73·4
Scotland	**15·1**	**24·1**	**74·5**

Source: Health and Wellbeing Profiles, Scotland Overview Report 2010 (adapted)

SOURCE C: (CONTINUED)

SOURCE C3   Percentage (%) Cigarette Smoking by Socio-Economic Group, Adults aged 16+

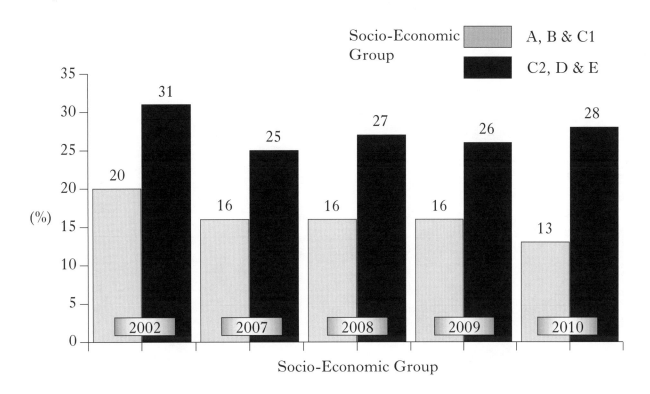

Source: Cancer UK website (adapted)

SOURCE C4   Percentage (%) Smoking Rate By Age, 2000–2010

Age \ Year	2000	2002	2004	2006	2008	2010
16–19	30	22	23	20	18	20
20–24	35	37	36	33	29	25
25–34	39	36	35	33	30	28
35–49	31	29	31	26	24	25
50–59	27	27	26	23	23	21
60+	16	17	15	13	13	13

Source: Cancer Research UK website (adapted)

SOURCE C: (CONTINUED)

SOURCE C5 Public Opinion Survey on Smoking in Scotland 2011. Figures in percentage (%)

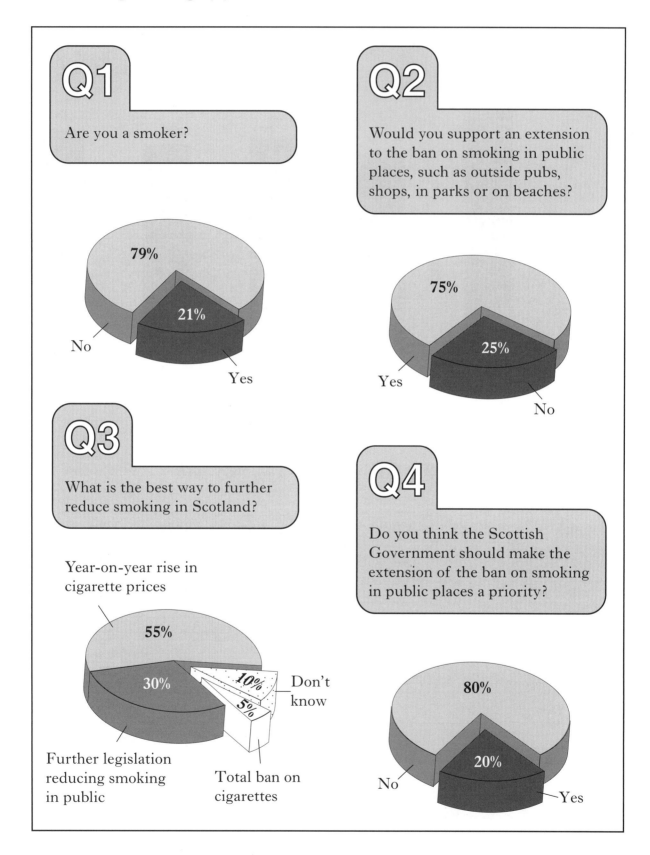

1101 people interviewed. Adapted from face-to-face survey across Scotland. January–March 2011

Marks

DECISION MAKING EXERCISE

QUESTIONS

Questions 1 to 4 are based on Sources A to C on pages 2–6. Answer Questions 1 to 4 before attempting Question 5.

In Questions 1 to 4, use <u>only</u> the Sources described in each question.

Question 1

Use **only** *Source C1 and Source A.*

Why might Carrie Brody be accused of exaggeration?   2

Question 2

Use **only** *Source C2, C3 and Source A.*

To what extent does the evidence support Carrie Brody?   3

Question 3

Use **only** *Source C4 and Source B.*

Why might Nick Matheson be accused of exaggeration?   2

Question 4

Use **only** *Source C5 and Source B.*

To what extent does the evidence support Nick Matheson?   3

(10)

Question 5

Marks

DECISION MAKING EXERCISE (DME)

You are a health advisor to the Scottish Government. You have been asked to prepare a report in which you recommend or reject a proposal (PASS—Protection Against Second-hand Smoking) which would make it illegal to smoke directly outside entrances to buildings used by the public and in Scotland's parks and on beaches.

Your answer should be written in a style appropriate to a report.

Your report should:

* recommend or reject the proposal (PASS—Protection Against Second-hand Smoking)

* provide arguments to support your decision

* identify and comment on any arguments which may be presented by those who oppose your decision

* refer to all the Sources provided

    AND

* **must** include relevant background knowledge.

The written and statistical sources which are provided are:

SOURCE A: PASS Will Improve Public Health

SOURCE B: Unnecessary Interference in People's Lives

SOURCE C: Statistical Information

(20)

Total: 30 marks

[END OF QUESTION PAPER]

HIGHER

2014

[BLANK PAGE]

X236/12/01

NATIONAL
QUALIFICATIONS
2014

TUESDAY, 29 APRIL
9.00 AM – 10.30 AM

MODERN STUDIES
HIGHER
Paper 1

Candidates should answer **FOUR** questions:

- **ONE** from Section A

and

- **ONE** from Section B

and

- **ONE** from Section C

and

ONE OTHER from <u>**EITHER**</u> Section A <u>**OR**</u> Section C

Section A: Political Issues in the United Kingdom

Section B: Social Issues in the United Kingdom

Section C: International Issues.

Each question is worth 15 marks.

SQA

SECTION A—Political Issues in the United Kingdom

Each question is worth 15 marks

STUDY THEME 1A: DEVOLVED DECISION MAKING IN SCOTLAND

Question A1

To what extent are Members of the Scottish Parliament (MSPs) effective in holding the Scottish Government to account?

STUDY THEME 1B: DECISION MAKING IN CENTRAL GOVERNMENT

Question A2

Assess the effectiveness of pressure groups in influencing decision making in Central Government.

STUDY THEME 1C: POLITICAL PARTIES AND THEIR POLICIES (INCLUDING THE SCOTTISH DIMENSION)

Question A3

There are few policy differences between the main political parties.

Discuss.

STUDY THEME 1D: ELECTORAL SYSTEMS, VOTING AND POLITICAL ATTITUDES

Question A4

The Single Transferable Vote (STV) provides for fairer representation than First Past the Post.

Discuss.

SECTION B—Social Issues in the United Kingdom
Each question is worth 15 marks

STUDY THEME 2: WEALTH AND HEALTH INEQUALITIES IN THE UNITED KINGDOM

EITHER

Question B5

To what extent does the Welfare State continue to meet its aims?

OR

Question B6

Critically examine the view that government in the UK has failed to reduce gender **and/or** race inequalities.

[Turn over for Section C on *Page four*

SECTION C—International Issues

Each question is worth 15 marks

STUDY THEME 3A: THE REPUBLIC OF SOUTH AFRICA

Question C7

Critically examine the view that inequalities are greater within racial groups than between racial groups.

STUDY THEME 3B: THE PEOPLE'S REPUBLIC OF CHINA

Question C8

Critically examine the view that economic success is benefiting all of the people of China.

STUDY THEME 3C: THE UNITED STATES OF AMERICA

Question C9

To what extent has immigration benefited the USA in recent years?

STUDY THEME 3D: THE EUROPEAN UNION

Question C10

To what extent has there been agreement between European Union members over reform of the Common Agricultural and Fisheries policies?

STUDY THEME 3E: THE POLITICS OF DEVELOPMENT IN AFRICA

Question C11

With reference to specific African countries (excluding the Republic of South Africa):

Trade is more important than foreign aid in promoting development in Africa.

Discuss.

STUDY THEME 3F: GLOBAL SECURITY

Question C12

Critically examine the view that NATO has an important part to play in achieving international peace and security.

[END OF QUESTION PAPER]

X236/12/02

NATIONAL
QUALIFICATIONS
2014

TUESDAY, 29 APRIL
10.50 AM – 12.05 PM

MODERN STUDIES
HIGHER
Paper 2

Summary of Decision Making Exercise

You are a health advisor to the Scottish Government. You have been asked to prepare a report in which you recommend or reject a proposal (*Fruitstart*) to provide vouchers to low-income parents to spend on fruit for their children.

Before beginning the DME Q5, you must answer a number of evaluating questions (Q1–4) based on the source material provided. The source material is:

SOURCE A: An Investment in the Next Generation

SOURCE B: A Waste of Taxpayers' Money

SOURCE C: Statistical Information

$\times$ SQA
©

SOURCE A: AN INVESTMENT IN THE NEXT GENERATION

Numerous reports show health statistics in Scotland improving but the health gap between the most and least affluent in society is an embarrassment. Across Scotland, the difference in life expectancy can be more than ten years. This is unacceptable. More must be done. Government has a responsibility to reduce health inequalities.

5   One way to reduce health inequality would be to introduce *Fruitstart*. *Fruitstart* is a proposal to improve children's health. *Fruitstart* is a targeted, means-tested initiative which focuses on the health needs of the poorest. It will provide low-income parents with a weekly £5 voucher that can only be spent on fruit. The voucher will be given only to those families who are already entitled to free school meals. As a nation, we

10 need to eat healthier and make better lifestyle choices. As children get older, year-on-year statistics prove that the number of young people regularly eating five fruits per day decreases. *Fruitstart*, once up and running, will sit alongside a number of Scottish government initiatives to improve health.

One of the main reasons for low fruit consumption is lack of availability. Convenience

15 stores in deprived areas, which may not currently stock the healthiest of foods, will now have an incentive to stock fresh fruit as there will be an increased demand for their products. Similarly, the barrier of affordability will be tackled. Some parents have a choice between buying fruit or buying junk food which fills hungry children up. Parents in deprived areas will no longer have to make this choice. £5 of fruit per week for each

20 child will kick-start a revolution in eating habits. Evidence suggests people who adopt healthy eating habits while young will continue to eat healthily as adults.

Fruitstart will help address one of the challenges facing the NHS—inappropriate lifestyle choices and their impact on health, including the problems associated with junk food and over consumption in our increasingly time-limited society. However, time

25 to prepare healthy meals is not necessarily the issue for parents living in low income households but the price of food does affect the choices they make. Although it is true that the majority of children are of a healthy weight, little wonder more than double the number of children are obese in the most deprived families compared to the least deprived. Forward looking government action has, in other areas, been successful in

30 changing lifestyle choices and improving health.

Fruitstart is a sensible use of taxpayers' money. Funds invested today will pay dividends for generations freeing up resources for other areas of government spending. Admittedly, the benefits of *Fruitstart* will not be seen straight away. Changes in health take time. However taken as part of a wide range of government health initiatives,

35 Scotland will continue to see life expectancy increase and health inequalities narrow.

Tanya Palmer, Health Campaigner

SOURCE B: A WASTE OF TAXPAYERS' MONEY

Fruitstart is another example of unnecessary government spending.   In 2014, the Scottish Government does not need another initiative to improve health. This is an insane suggestion which will be met with ridicule not just by the hard working taxpayer but by the very people it is designed to help. In a period of economic restraint, the
5 Scottish Government should not be looking to increase spending.   Funding to reduce inequalities for the early years and young people is already one of Scottish Government's biggest areas of expenditure. Schools spend vast resources promoting healthy eating. *Fruitstart* sounds like another initiative which will cost a lot of money but will make no difference to health inequalities.

10 It is the individual's responsibility to look after their own health. If people choose to ignore government advice, that is their choice. *Fruitstart* will actually do more harm than good. Once again, it gives out the message that if you do not take responsibility for your life, the State will do it for you. If you don't work hard at school to get a good education, the State will provide benefits for you. If you choose to squander those
15 benefits on unhealthy food for your children, the State will provide healthy food. The only way health in this country will improve is when people learn to take responsibility for their own lives.

It is true that the Welfare State needs modernising. What is needed is to support those who work hard, play by the rules and pay their taxes. Scotland now has a generation
20 of people who have never worked and who expect the State to provide for their every need. Hardworking people are expected to pay an ever greater share of their income supporting the 'workshy'. This is completely unfair and totally unsustainable. Public opinion may agree that government has a responsibility to promote healthy eating but with child poverty rates predicted to fall in the future there really won't be any need
25 for *Fruitstart*. Sensibly, and not before time, the UK Government has already made changes to the benefit system with the aim of reducing the UK's 'dependency culture'.

Government action which aims to influence the choices made by individuals does not work. Children have always eaten unhealthy foods. *Fruitstart* will not change the amount of fruit children eat. What's missing is open space for children and young
30 people to play and affordable local sports facilities. The millions spent on *Fruitstart* would be better spent on sports facilities which are sadly lacking, especially in poorer communities. The spirit of the Olympics and Commonwealth Games needs to be supported by quality facilities available for all young people. If children and young people are motivated to keep fit, their diet will look after itself.

Calvin McKenzie, Newspaper Columnist

[Turn over for Source C on *Pages four*, *five* and *six*

SOURCE C: STATISTICAL INFORMATION

SOURCE C1 **Percentage (%) Daily Fruit Consumption, Scottish Children by Age, 2010**

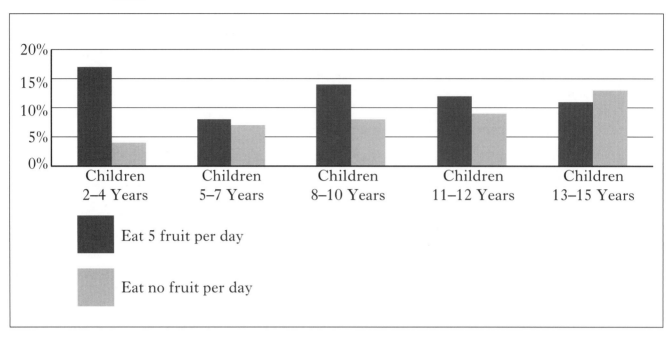

Source: Adapted from Scottish Government website

SOURCE C2 **Selected Information Scottish Children 2012**

Weight	Underweight	Healthy Weight	Overweight	Obese	Morbidly Obese
Children aged 5–15 years old	2%	76%	13%	4%	5%

Exercise	Age 5–7 years	Age 8–10 years	Age 11–12 years	Age 13–15 years
Percentage of children completing 60 minutes physical activity per day	75%	76%	67%	55%

Poverty	Least deprived families	Most deprived families
Percentage of children obese	7%	11%
Percentage of children who eat chips 2+ times per week	42%	69%

Source: Adapted from Scottish Government website

Page four

SOURCE C: (CONTINUED)

SOURCE C3 Scottish Government funding for reducing health inequalities 2008/09 to 2010/11 in millions of pounds (£ millions)

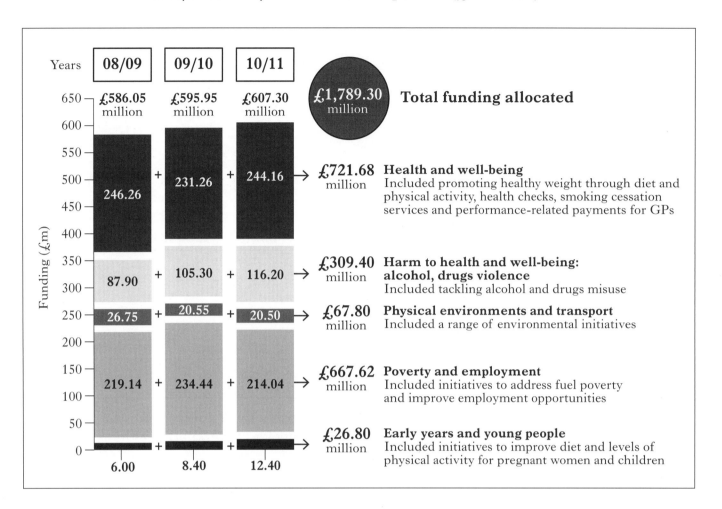

Source: Adapted from Audit Scotland website and 'Equally Well: Report of the Ministerial Task Force on Health Inequalities', by the Scottish Government, 2008 © Crown Copyright.

SOURCE C: (CONTINUED)

SOURCE C4   Percentage (%) UK Child Poverty Rates 1980–2020 (projected)

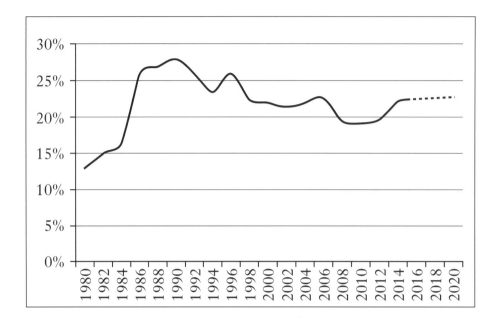

Source: Child Poverty Action Group

SOURCE C5   Public Opinion Survey January 2014

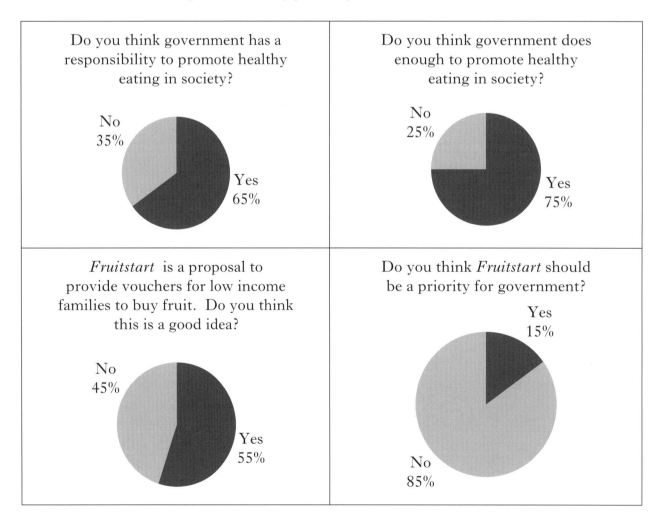

Source: Telephone survey, 1011 people interviewed, January 2014 (adapted)

Marks

DECISION MAKING EXERCISE

QUESTIONS

Questions 1 to 4 are based on Sources A to C on pages 2–6. Answer Questions 1 to 4 before attempting Question 5.

In Questions 1 to 4, use <u>only</u> the Sources described in each question.

Question 1

*Use **only** Source C1 and Source A.*

Why might Tanya Palmer be accused of exaggeration?

2

Question 2

*Use **only** Source C2 and Source A.*

To what extent does the evidence support Tanya Palmer?

3

Question 3

*Use **only** Source C3 and Source B.*

Why might Calvin McKenzie be accused of exaggeration?

2

Question 4

*Use **only** Source C4, C5 and Source B.*

To what extent does the evidence support Calvin McKenzie?

3

(10)

Question 5

Marks

DECISION MAKING EXERCISE (DME)

You are a health advisor to the Scottish Government. You have been asked to prepare a report in which you recommend or reject a proposal (*Fruitstart*) to provide vouchers to low-income parents to spend on fruit for their children.

Your answer should be written in a style appropriate to a report.

Your report should:

• recommend or reject the proposal to provide vouchers to low-income parents to spend on fruit for their children

• provide arguments to support your recommendation

• identify and comment on any arguments which may be presented by those who oppose your recommendation

• refer to all the Sources provided

    AND

• **must** include relevant background knowledge.

The written and statistical sources which are provided are:

SOURCE A: An Investment in the Next Generation

SOURCE B: A Waste of Taxpayers' Money

SOURCE C: Statistical Information

(20)

Total: 30 marks

[END OF QUESTION PAPER]

[BLANK PAGE]

Acknowledgements

Permission has been sought from all relevant copyright holders and Hodder Gibson is grateful for the use of the following:

Two tables 'Male and female death rates by selected causes in Scotland, 2003–2007' and 'Male and female life expectancy at birth in Scotland, 2005' © Crown copyright. Data supplied by General Register Office for Scotland. Contains public sector information licensed under the Open Government Licence v2.0 (2010 Paper 2 page 4);

Two graphs taken from East Glasgow Well Man Clinics Final Evaluation Report, September 2006 (2010 Paper 2 page 6);

The graph 'Numbers of people in the UK on low incomes in millions 1979–2009' taken from The Poverty Site, www.poverty.org.uk © Guy Palmer (2011 Paper 2 page 4);

The graph 'Comparison of the relative value of the national minimum wage in Pounds (£s) between selected developed countries, 2008' adapted from the Low Pay Commission Report 2009 © Low Pay Commission (2011 Paper 2 page 4);

The graph 'Percentage (%) of households in poverty in selected EU countries 2009', adapted from Eurostat, © European Communities, 2009 (2011 Paper 2 page 5);

A graph adapted from Labour Force Survey, Office for National Statistics © Crown Copyright. Contains public sector information licensed under the Open Government Licence v2.0 (2011 Paper 2 page 6);

The graph 'Percentage (%) of students on degree courses from working-class backgrounds at selected Scottish universities 2008–09.' Adapted from Higher Education Statistics Agency (2012 Paper 2 page 4);

The graph 'Percentage (%) of individuals in selected professional occupations who attended fee-paying private schools'. Adapted from http://www.cabinetoffice.gov.uk/media/227102/fair-access.pdf. Contains public sector information licensed under the Open Government Licence v2.0 (2012 Paper 2 page 5);

The table 'Views of young people in percentage (%) on best way government could help them enter a professional career in percentage (%)'. Adapted from http://www.cabinetoffice.gov.uk/media/213698/national_youth_survey.pdf. Contains public sector information licensed under the Open Government Licence v2.0 (2012 Paper 2 page 5);

The table 'Percentage (%) of students from working-class backgrounds at UK universities by course choice (selected) 2008–09.' Adapted from Higher Education Statistics Agency (2012 Paper 2 page 5);

The graph 'Median* full-time earnings (£s) by occupation in Scotland, 2009. Taken from 'Annual Survey of Hours and Earnings', Office for National Statistics. Contains public sector information licensed under the Open Government Licence v2.0 (2012 Paper 2 page 6);

Statistics taken from WHO, Health in the European Union, 2009 (2013 Paper 2 page 4);

Statistics taken from Scottish Public Health Observatory (2013 Paper 2 page 4);

Statistics taken from Cancer UK website (2013 Paper 2 page 5);

Statistics taken from Cancer UK website (2013 Paper 2 page 6);

Statistics adapted from Scottish Government website (http://scotland.gov.uk/Publications/2011/09/27084018/39). Contains public sector information licensed under the Open Government Licence v2.0 (2014 Paper 2 page 4); (2014 Paper 2 page 4);

Information taken from: http://www.scotland.gov.uk/Publications/2012/05/5385/5. Contains public sector information licensed under the Open Government Licence v2.0 (2014 Paper 2 page 4);

Graph by Audit Scotland, based on figures taken from p49 of 'Equally Well: Report of the Ministerial Task Force on Health Inequalities', by the Scottish Government, 2008 (http://www.audit-scotland.gov.uk/docs/health/2012/nr_121213_health_inequalities) © Crown Copyright. Contains public sector information licensed under the Open Government Licence v2.0 (2014 Paper 2 page 5);

Graph © Child Poverty Action Group (2014 Paper 2 page 6).

SQA HIGHER
MODERN STUDIES 2010–2014

MODERN STUDIES HIGHER
PAPER 1
2010

Section A – Political Issues in the United Kingdom

Study Theme 1A – Devolved Decision Making in Scotland

Question A1

"Pass" and better answers should feature developed, exemplified knowledge and understanding of:

The part played by Scottish representatives at Westminster
The debate surrounding Scotland's future with regard to the union
And
Balanced comment/analysis on whether Scottish representation is needed at Westminster.
Answers may refer to:

- The role of Scotland's 59 MPs, the Scottish Office (part of the Ministry for Justice) and the Secretary of State for Scotland (2009 Jim Murphy) in representing Scotland's interests at Westminster.
- The devolved (health, education, transport, etc.) and reserved (constitutional matters, social security, foreign policy, etc.) powers. Most legislation affecting Scotland is passed in the Scottish Parliament although the UK Parliament at Westminster remains sovereign.
- The number of Scottish-based MPs in the 2009 UK Cabinet (18%) inc. Prime Minister Gordon Brown and Chancellor of the Exchequer Alistair Darling.
- Criticism of rising cost of Scotland Office and there have been calls to scrap post of Secretary of State for Scotland. First meeting of Secretary of State for Scotland and SNP Ministers in June 2009.
- Legislation including phased abolition of prescription charges, freezing of Council Tax, abolition of graduate endowment fee, ban on smoking in enclosed public places, etc.
- The calls for increased powers for the Scottish Parliament including greater fiscal independence, control over nuclear power and weapons based in Scotland, control of elections, fishing industry, etc. Renaming of Scottish Executive as the Scottish Government.
- The West Lothian Question and responses. The Conservatives Democracy Task Force argued for English MP only votes on English only laws but incorporating English-only Committee and Report stages but a vote of all MPs at Second and Third Readings. Cameron has talked of an 'English grand committee'.
- The SNP's 'National Conversation' and proposal for a referendum on Scotland's constitutional future and the pro-union parties Scottish Constitutional Commission (led by Sir Kenneth Calman) which was tasked to review devolution (but not independence). Calman's proposals for greater fiscal powers and control over speed limits, drink driving laws and elections in Scotland.
- The on-going debate over the Barnett Formula and/or the future effects of Barnett.
- Increased use of Legislative Consent Motions (formerly Sewell Motions).

- Recent calls for greater devolution of power following MPs expenses scandal.
- Other relevant points.

Study Theme 1B - Decision Making in Central Government

Question A2

"Pass" and better answers should feature developed, exemplified knowledge and understanding of:

Opportunities for Parliament (HoC) and (HoL) to control the Executive
Extent to which Parliament has been able to control the Executive
And
Balanced comment/analysis on the view that Parliament has little control over the Executive.

Answers may refer to:
- For full marks an answer should make reference to the House of Lords.
- Parliament has two functions: one legislative the other to scrutinise the work of the Executive. There is a view that Parliament has become less effective in holding the Executive to account in recent years.
- Debates in the House of Commons Chamber (and Westminster Hall) including those held within the legislative process (eg Second Reading, Report Stage and Third Reading). Debates also take place during the Committee stage of bills (usually in General Committees rather than in House of Commons). Also, Adjournment Debate – half hour at the end of the day's business and Opposition Days (around 20 days) when opposition parties set agenda.
- House of Lords debates include those also within legislative process and general debates that are held on Thursdays. There are also many short debates of up to 90 minutes on days when legislation is being considered or at the end of the day's business.
- Votes in HoC. Government defeated over plan to restrict rights of Ghurkas to settle in UK (04/09) and plan to hold votes across England (06/09). Government forced to bring compensation package after abolition of 10p tax rate.
- Votes in the HoL. Government defeated in Nov. 2008 over issue of keeping people's DNA and fingerprints on the police national database; in Oct. 2008 over extension to length of time terrorist suspect could be held without charge (from 28 to 42 days) and in June '09 over donations to political parties from tax exiles.
- Parliament Acts state that HoL cannot delay (in view of Speaker) money bills (taxes/public spending) for more than one month or public bills for more than two parliamentary sessions or one calendar year. These provisions only apply to bills that originate in the House of Commons.
- 'Sailsbury Convention' where Lords does not oppose legislation proposed in Government's election manifesto.
- Work of Select Committees which examine the work of the main government departments in terms of expenditure, administration and policy and Public bill committees (formerly standing committees) which examine legislation.
- Question Time – Begins business of Commons four times per week. PMQT is on Wednesday's for 30 minutes.
- Size of Government majority. Can work two ways: small majority may help to maintain party discipline whereas large majority may encourage rebellions eg over part privatisation of Royal Mail (plans later shelved).

- Use of the Whip.
- Calls for widespread reform of Parliament inc. reduction in Executive power after recent expenses/cash for amendments scandals.
- Rare threat of vote of no confidence.
- Other relevant points.

Study Theme 1C - Political Parties and their Policies (including the Scottish Dimension)

Question A3

"Pass" and better answers should feature developed, exemplified knowledge and understanding of:

Ways in which different political parties decide policy
Extent of influence of party members in deciding policy in different parties
And
Balanced comment/analysis of the extent to which party members decide their party's policies.

Answers may refer to:
- For full marks answers must refer to more than one political party.

Conservative Party/Scottish Conservative Party
- Traditionally policy making decided by leadership but reformed under Hague.
- National Conservative Convention and Conservative Political Forum allow party members to have input into policy but they remain advisory. Cameron has indicated that he is in support of the ideas, more policy to be decided by party members locally. Challenge Groups and Taskforces set up to allow party members opportunity to contribute.
- Direct ballots of party membership on selected issues but issues closely controlled by leadership as individual members cannot initiate own proposals or ballots.

Labour Party/Scottish Labour Party
- Labour Party consists of Constituency Labour Parties, affiliated trade unions, socialist societies and the Co-operative Party with which it has an electoral agreement. Members who are elected to parliamentary positions take part in the Parliamentary Labour Party (PLP).
- Party's decision-making bodies at a national level formally include the National Executive Committee (NEC), Labour Party Conference and National Policy Forum (NPF) although in practice the parliamentary leadership has the final say on policy.
- The Labour Party Constitution states that Party policies making up the Labour Party programme should be approved by the Conference, subject to receiving two thirds support. The election manifesto, which consists of policies from the programme, has to be agreed between the parliamentary leadership and the NEC.
- Leadership/NEC proposes programme and conference votes to support/reject programme with CLPs, affiliated organisations and trade unions having weighting according to number of members.
- Policy in the Labour Party is made through a process called Partnership in Power (PiP) which is designed to involve all party stakeholders (inc. ordinary party members). PiP does this through a rolling programme of policy development and a year-round dialogue between the party and government. Development of policy is carried out by six policy commissions.

Liberal Democrats/Scottish Liberal Democrats
- Policy making body is the Federal Conference. Twice a year, in spring and autumn, elected representatives from the Liberal Democrat constituency parties assemble at the party conference to establish federal party policy. Representatives from every local party, organised around parliamentary constituencies, are elected to attend federal conference.
- Conference decides policy matters on national and 'English' issues; separate Scottish Liberal Democrat Party makes policy decisions on Scottish issues.
- Every two years, conference representatives elect a Federal Policy Committee (FPC) which is responsible for the production of the policy papers that are debated at Conference, and is responsible for election manifestos. Party members discuss policy papers in local and regional meetings, and their representatives then debate and vote on policy motions and papers at Conference. Conference also debates motions submitted by local parties and conference representatives.

Scottish National Party
- Members can submit motions on policy and national strategy to be discussed by the party at national level.
- Local branches are drawn together to form a Constituency Association. Branches and CAs send representatives to the two national bodies that agree the policies of the Party – The National Council and Annual National Conference. Annual Conference is the supreme governing body of the Party and elects the National Executive Committee, the leadership of the Party, which deals with the day-to-day running of its affairs.
- Credit candidates who make comparisons between parties as to the extent to which party members decide policies.
- Credit candidates who appreciate decision making structures within parties change when in office.
- Other relevant points.

Study Theme 1D – Electoral Systems, Voting and Political Attitudes

Question A4

"Pass" and better answers should feature developed, exemplified knowledge and understanding of:

The main features of the STV and FPTP electoral systems
The effect of the STV and the FPTP electoral systems on the way that voters are represented
And
Balanced comment/analysis of whether STV provides for better representation than FPTP.

Answers may refer to:
STV
- First used in Scotland for Scottish local government elections of May 2007.
- Large multi-member constituencies.
- Voters list candidates in order of preference within, as well as between, parties.
- To gain election, candidates are required to gain a pre-determined quota of votes. Where this does not happen, the second, third, etc, preference of voters is used until all the representatives are elected.

FPTP
- Used for UK Parliament elections.
- Simple majority system.
- Candidate with most votes wins; party with most MPs forms the government.
- STV is a system of proportional representation (PR) so notionally fairer.
- Claim that few votes are 'wasted' under STV and that almost every voter gets at least partial representation.

- No need for tactical voting.
- Voters can choose between candidates both within and between parties; can express preferences between the abilities/attributes of individual candidates.
- Scottish local election results of 2007 saw only two councils have single-party administrations, Glasgow and North Lanarkshire. Labour's majority on Glasgow City Council fell from 64 to 11.
- Most local government administrations are made up of coalitions (21 of 32 Scottish councils have more than one party in the administration). As a result there has been an increase in 'compromise politics' which is not necessarily better representation.
- STV gives more opportunity for voters to choose female or minority ethnic candidates but local political parties continue to decide who stands for their party.
- STV breaks the direct link between voters and individual representative but it is argued that accountability has increased, and through this better representation, as there is no such thing as a safe seat. The Electoral Reform Society Scotland argues that councillors are more visible, more approachable and working harder as a consequence of STV's introduction.
- Recent debate over PR for Westminster.
- FPTP retains close representative-constituency link and usually produces majority government.
- Other relevant points.

Section B – Social Issues in the United Kingdom

Study Theme 2 – Wealth and Health Inequalities in the United Kingdom

Question B5

"Pass" and better answers should feature developed, exemplified knowledge and understanding of:

Lifestyle choices and their effect on health
Other factors which impact on health
And
Balanced comment/analysis on the impact of lifestyle choices on health.

Answers may refer to:
- Evidence of health inequalities expressed in terms of life expectancy, mortality and morbidity rates, etc.
- Evidence may be drawn from wide range of reports eg 'Equally Well: Report of Ministerial Task Force 2008' or 'Inequalities in Health 1981-2001' published in 2007, Scottish Household Survey, etc.
- Lifestyle choices: smoking, alcohol consumption, diet, use of illegal drugs, extent of exercise, uptake of preventative care services, etc., are factors that impact on health.
- Poorest groups/people in poorest areas make worst life style choices ie smoke more and have higher alcohol consumption; more likely to use illegal drugs; take less exercise; have poorer diets and make less use of preventative health care.
- Other factors that affect good health:
  - Local environment – quality of housing, community facilities, extent of crime, etc.
  - Individual circumstances – income levels, unemployment, single parent, carer, age, etc.
  - Gender.
  - Type/nature of employment – professional, labourer, stress of work, etc.
  - Quality of, and access to, local health care services.
  - Hereditary/biological factors.
- Even allowing for individual lifestyle choices, poorest groups still far more likely to die younger (between eight and ten years) and experience poorer health than those in wealthiest groups. Countries with lower income inequalities have a lower health gap.
- Other relevant points.

Question B6

"Pass" and better answers should feature developed, exemplified knowledge and understanding of:
- Government policies to reduce gender and/or ethnic inequalities
- Impact of government policies

And
Balanced comment on/analysis of the extent to which government policies have reduced gender and/or ethnic inequalities.

Answers may refer to:
- Equal Pay Act (1970); Sex Discrimination Act (1975) and Sex Discrimination Regulations (2008); Equality Act (2006); The Commission for Equality and Human Rights (2007); Gender Equality Duty Code of Practice (2007) places legal responsibility on public authorities to demonstrate that they treat men and women fairly; Women's Enterprise Task Force (2006); Equality Bill 2008 includes provision that forces companies to publish pay rates.
- Work and Families Act (2006) extended the right to request flexible working; extended further 2009.
- CTC and Working Tax Credit. Government sees affordable childcare ('wraparound childcare') as crucial to narrowing the wage gap.
- Minimum Wage has disproportionately benefited women and minorities. Maternity and paternity leave.
- Skills Strategy (2003) to address the fact that over 50% of women in part time work are working below their skill level.
- Race Relations Acts; Race Relations (Amendment) Act, 2000.
- Ethnic Minority Employment Task Force (2004) to tackle unemployment among black and Asian people.
- One Scotland.
- Women now make up 60% of the university population; success of women in reaching senior posts varies from place to place. Glass ceiling only cracked, not broken. Women make up 46% of all millionaires and are expected to own 60% of the UK's wealth by 2010.
- Women make up only 19.3% of MPs, less than 10% of the senior judiciary, national newspaper editors and senior police officers; only 11% of directors in FTSE 100 firms are women despite accounting for over half of the UK population and 46% of the labour force.
- Sex and Power Report 2007.
- Gender pay gap: UK women in full time work earn 12.8% less per hour than men (2009). Gender pay gap has widened in some cases in recent years. Pay gap higher in the private sector than in the public sector. Higher women rise up the pay ladder, the greater pay gap becomes.
- Occupational segregation.
- In 2008 National Audit Office found the employment rate for ethnic minority population was 60% compared to 74% in general population. This gap had narrowed by only 1.3% in 20 years.
- Growing evidence of a 'race pay gap' which sees black and Asian workers earn up to 15% less than white counter parts.
- Only 4.3% of board members are from ethnic minority groups despite accounting for 8.5% of workforce ('Race for Opportunity').
- Women from Black Caribbean, Pakistani and Bangladeshi groups most likely to face a higher risk of unemployment, lower pay and have fewer prospects for promotion. EOC's 'Moving on up?' report 2007.

- References to health policies and success or otherwise in reducing gender and race inequalities will be credited.
- Other relevant points.

Section C – International Issues

Study Theme 3A – The Republic of South Africa

Question C7

"Pass" and better answers should feature developed, exemplified knowledge and understanding of:

Main features of South African political system
Extent to which different parties are represented in South African politics
And
Balanced comment/analysis on the extent to which South Africa is a multi-party democracy.

Answers may refer to:
- South Africa is a constitutional democracy with a three-tier system of government.
- Federal state with nine provincial governments; each province elects a provincial legislature consisting of between 30 and 80 members. These legislatures have the power to raise provincial taxes and make laws.
- Bicameral parliament elected every five years, comprising the 400 seat National Assembly and the 90-seat National Council of Provinces with the NCOP consisting of 54 permanent members and 36 special delegates.
- Local government elected for 4 years; 284 metropolitan, district and local municipalities.
- Party List electoral system (200 from national party lists and 200 from party list in each of nine provinces).
- 13 political groups represented in National Assembly.
- The President is elected by the National Assembly. Under the SA Constitution, the President is permitted to serve a maximum of two five-year terms. Jacob Zuma elected President in May 2009. There is also a Deputy President.
- Constitution guarantees many rights including property rights and education; two-thirds of members of Parliament and at least 6 provinces need to support change to Constitution – ANC support in NA falls just short of this (65.9%).
- Success of ANC nationally and at provincial level since 1999 but support fell in 2009. Impact of Cope and gains for DA. Decline of IFP.
- In 2009 national election percentage of votes: ANC – 65.9%; DA – 16.6%; Cope – 7.4%.; IFP – 4.5%.
- ANC won majority in 8 of 9 provinces. DA won majority in W. Cape (22 of 44 seats).
- Seats in National Assembly 2009 were: ANC = 264 (-33 from 2004); DA = 67 (+20); Cope = 30 (new); IFP = 18 (−5). Altogether there are 13 parties represented in NA. 28 parties contested 2009 election.
- In 2006 local elections ANC polled the most votes in each of nine provinces (although lost position of power in Cape Town).
- After 2009 election DA had representation in all provinces.
- Effectiveness of opposition parties – arguably still somewhat fragmented and divided. Some evidence ANC tolerates opposition rather than respects.
- Concerns about ANC intolerance towards media opposition.
- Other relevant points.

Study Theme 3B – The People's Republic of China

Question C8

"Pass" and better answers should feature developed, exemplified knowledge and understanding of:

Sources of opposition to the Chinese Communist Party (CPC)
Extent of opposition within China as a whole
And
Balanced comment/analysis on the extent of opposition to the Communist Party in China.

Answers may refer to:
- Dissidents eg Hu Jia who was sent to prison for 3.5 years ahead of Olympic Games but few in number.
- Minorities eg Xinjiang and Tibet and related separatist movements. At least 140 people killed in rioting in Xinjiang (July '09).
- Provinces eg Guangdong has a reputation of not following central government directives.
- Hong Kong: 'One China Two Systems' and Taiwan's continued detachment from China. Former Hong Kong Governor Chris Patten sees China as threat to 'democracy' (11/08).
- Poor, unemployed/under-employed, landless. Up to 20m migrants forced to return to countryside as result of downturn in economy.
- Rise in levels of web-based dissent eg through blogs and chatrooms. High number of journalists under arrest but BBC website recently unblocked. Internationally China ranked very poorly in terms of internet/media freedom. Charter '08 document and on-line petition.
- Middle classes who have gained economic power and social status but no real political power.
- Crackdown on protest before and during Olympic Games.
- Numerous local and environmental protests involving crowds of up to 30,000. There were a total of 120,000 "mass incidents' in 2008. 2009 expected to be higher (20 years since Tiananmen Sq. protests/50 years of CPC rule).
- Greater criticism allowed of corrupt local officials. Renewed crackdown after Sichuan earthquake. Reaction to contaminated milk scandal.
- No general opposition to CPC; marginalised and disparate. Rises in the general standard of living have reduced criticism of CPC. Consensus is that there is little demand for political change.
- There are eight other political parties in China but are not in opposition to the CPC. Parties may participate in Government decisions but not allowed formal organisational status so can't raise funds or campaign.
- No free trade union association. ACFTU seen as tool of CPC.
- Treatment of members of Falun Gong.
- Wide range of powers available to Chinese authorities to silence political protestors. Arrest, imprisonment, house arrest, etc. Catch-all subversion, sedition and leaking of State secrets laws.
- Other relevant points.

Study Theme 3C – The United States of America

Question C9

"Pass" and better answers should feature developed, exemplified knowledge and understanding of:

The US immigration debate
The impact of immigration on US society (economic, social, political, cultural, regional)
And
Balanced comment/analysis on the impact overall of immigration on the USA.

Answers may refer to:
- US reputation as 'land of free' and history of immigration. Ethnic diversity is cause for celebration.
- Argument that immigrants stimulate the economy in terms of demand for housing, medical care, education and other services.
- Immigrants do many of the low paid jobs that Americans do not want; wages are suppressed and this keeps the US

competitive. Many authorities in larger US cities have instructed enforcement personnel to not comply with federal agencies with regard to illegal immigrants in their jurisdiction.

- Most economists believe immigrants contribute more in the long-term than they cost to assimilate. Most immigrants are young, economically active and often skilled.
- Bush's 'Guest Worker' program attempted to recognise economic benefits of immigration by allowing US employers to sponsor non-US citizens, failed in Congress. Arizona (and other SW States) is considering setting up its own 'guest worker program'. Congress has tried and failed three times to pass an immigration bill.
- Argument that wages levels are forced down by immigrants. There is competition in employment, for housing, etc. Some economists argue that immigration benefits middle class most but hurts poor.
- Cost to US taxpayer for health care, education and welfare payments. 33% use at least one welfare program compared to 19% native.
- 'US culture' being overwhelmed. English no longer main language in many areas. Hispanics majority forecast in California by 2030. In 2008, there was an estimated 11-12m illegal immigrants in the US (30% rise since 2000 but numbers now falling). Many immigrants make no attempt to assimilate.
- In 2007, 37m people in the US were immigrants (1 in 8 of total population with 1 in 3 illegals). Over 1m people became US citizens in 2008.
- Huge investment in US border security; tighter restrictions on legal immigration. Obama plans to increase border security further. Various States have attempted to reduce access to welfare payments, etc. to illegal immigrants.
- Polls show most in US in favour of tighter controls. Hardening of attitudes especially post 9/11. Patriot Act (and renewal) makes it easier for US authorities to deny access to 'aliens'. Anti-immigration groups eg 'Minuteman'.
- Increase in size of minority ethnic vote and importance in 2008 US Presidential election. Nearly 70% of Hispanics voted for Obama.
- Other relevant points.

Study Theme 3D – The European Union

Question C10

"Pass" and better answers should feature developed, exemplified knowledge and understanding of:

The aims and structures of the CAP/CFP
Impact of both the CAP and CFP on EU member states
And
Balanced comment/analysis on the extent to which the CAP/CFP has benefited the member states of the European Union.

Answers may refer to:
- CAP – aims to secure food supplies, increase production and productivity, reduce dependency on imported food, stabilise prices, secure farms incomes and increase the overall standard of living of all those involved in agriculture.
- Seen as more favourable to some: France gets most out of CAP overall (20%); Ireland and Greece do best on per capita terms. Biggest farmers gain most. 80% of funds go to just 20% of farmers.
- Implications of enlargement especially cost. UK wants to end direct farm payments by 2015-2020 leaving the CAP aimed at protecting the environment.
- Has produced huge food surpluses over the years; cost of storage/destruction.

- 2009 cost EU €56bn; 43% of budget but falling proportionally since 1985; agricultural spending to be steady between 2006-13 despite increased EU membership; support given to farmers in older members States will be cut 8-9%.
- Only 5% of EU citizens work in agriculture (18% in Poland) producing 1.6% of EU's GDP; but proportion falling; halved in 15 older member states between 1980 and 2003.
- New member states get subsidies but only at 25% of rate of older member states.
- Price support subsidies falling as farmers increasingly given direct payments. Cereal farmers paid to take land out of cultivation. Rural development aid paid as an alternative to encourage rural farm diversification. Reforms in 2003/4 led to payments linked to food safety, animal welfare and environmental protection. Rural development funding to increase. Aim to cut export subsidies.
- CFP – adopted in 1983; reformed in 1992 and 2002 with the aim of preserving fish stocks and the fishing industry. Needed to combat overfishing, improve fishermen's incomes, preserve marine ecosystems and maintain supply of fish to European markets.
- Fishing less than 1% of EU's GDP; in 2007-13 states have €3.8bn to spend with member states deciding how their allocation will be spent; emphasis to be on fish stock recovery plans, inland fishing and aquaculture.
- Member states are each given a national quota (total allowable catches – TACs). This is decided by Council of Ministers.
- To limit the capture of small fish so that they can reproduce, technical rules have been adopted. Minimum mesh sizes have been fixed. Certain areas may be closed to protect fish stocks. Some fishing gears can be banned and more "selective" techniques, which facilitate the escape of young fish and limit the capture of other species, may be made compulsory. Minimum fish sizes are set, below which it is illegal to land fish. Catches and landings have to be recorded in special logbooks.
- Enforcement – the authorities in the Member States have to ensure that CFP rules are respected. There is also a Community Inspectorate. Their role is to ensure that all national enforcement authorities apply the same standards of quality and fairness in their enforcement however, enforcement criticised for not preventing landing of illegal catches ('blackfish'), and the abuse of use of quotas ('quota hopping').
- CFP unpopular with fishing communities which, it is argued, has not maintained fishing stocks. SNP wants an end to EU control over fisheries.
- Entrenched interests in Spain, France, Portugal and Greece have successfully resisted reform of CFP.
- In 2009, EU Commission reported that the EU had too many fishing boats and major cuts were needed to make fishing sustainable. In a Green Paper the Commission stated fishermen should also be given more responsibility for managing stocks as well as asking for ideas for a reformed CFP in 2013.
- Other relevant points.

Study Theme 3E – The Politics of Development in Africa

Question C11

"Pass" and better answers should feature developed, exemplified knowledge and understanding of:

The part played by the UN in promoting development in Africa
The factors that limit UN programmes in promoting development
And
Balanced comment/analysis on the extent to which the UN has been effective in promoting development.

Answers may refer to:

- The UNDP and Progress towards the Millennium Development Goals (MDG) of 2015.
- The UN agencies and their roles:
  - WHO: promotion of health is seen as crucial to development. Examples include eradication of polio with mass vaccination programme in Somalia, Kenya and Ethiopia. 3m children under 5 vaccinated.
  - UNESCO: promotion of education is also seen as crucial to successful long-term development.
  - ILO: aims to promote rights at work, encourage decent employment and enhance social protection.
  - UNFPA aims to reduce poverty and ensure that every person enjoys a life of health and opportunity.
  - UNIDO helps developing countries and economies in transition.
  - FAO and IFAD work to reduce hunger by giving direct support, sharing information and expertise, and undertaking research to improve food supplies.
  - World Food Programme (WFP).
- UNICEF – is not funded by UN but relies on donations. Works closely with UN agencies in responding to crises and promoting development.
- Co-operation between the IMF, the World Bank, the WTO and the UN to promote development.
- Partnerships with voluntary organisations.
- Extent of and access to fresh water supplies and impact on health. UN Development Report of 2006 states it will be 2040 before MDG for fresh water supply reached in sub-Saharan Africa.
- FAO reported a rise in the numbers (265m) of hungry in sub-Saharan Africa in 2009. Impact of rising food prices and lower employment levels.
- Extent of available health care. Long-tem health problems created by malaria infection, HIV/AIDS, etc., affect the most economically active section of the population and slow development.
- MDG 2 (education provision) likely to be missed by 15 countries by 2015. Explanation of role of education in breaking the 'poverty cycle'.
- Climate change and impact on agriculture in marginal areas. Prediction that some staple foods eg maize production will decrease by 30% in future. Mismanagement of soil.
- Conflict. 20 major conflicts in Africa since 1960. In 2009, 13 countries affected eg Darfur. Huge obstacle to development – destruction and death, disruption to food supplies, financial cost, etc.
- Debt. G8 has cancelled debts of poorest 14 countries (estimated $200bn) but African countries still repay more in debt than receive in aid.
- Terms of world trade including price fluctuations affecting cash crops. Dumping of subsidised farm produce on local markets. Import tariffs and restrictions. Impact of 'Credit Crunch'.
- Corruption and land tenure issues eg Zimbabwe and collapse of economy. Legacy of colonisation.
- Political instability, military coups (DR of Congo) and economic mismanagement eg commentators have questioned the sustainability of Uganda's Poverty Eradication Action Plan.
- Divided views within UN membership towards best way forward; failure of many developed countries to give 0.7% of GNP to UN.
- Effect of natural disasters eg floods or drought.
- Other relevant points.

Study Theme 3F – Global Security

Question C12

"Pass" and better answers should feature developed, exemplified knowledge and understanding of:

The role of NATO

Extent to which NATO has been effective in achieving international peace and security

And

Balanced comment/analysis on the effectiveness of NATO in achieving international peace and security.

Answers may refer to:

- NATO has ensured W. Europe/Europe's security since 1949. Idea of 'collective defence' still relevant to existing, new and would-be members eg Ukraine. Membership has increased to 28 (Albania and Croatia 2009) and there are partnership agreements with many other countries eg Montenegro, which provide opportunities for defence co-operation.
- NATO provides forum for discussion of global issues which can reduce tension.
- Strategy of 'flexible response' adopted for 21st Century. Aims to deal with new crises both within and outwith North Atlantic area including ethnic violence, abuse of human rights, political instability, the spread of nuclear technology, terrorism and international crime.
- In 2002, NATO-Russia Council established to provide a framework for consultation on security issues.
- Peacemaking and peacekeeping roles (alongside EU or UN personnel) in Europe: Bosnia (IFOR/SFOR ended 2004); Kosovo (KFOR 1999 to present – 10,000 troops deployed 2009) and Macedonia (from 2001 to 2003).
- NATO had no direct role in Iraq but an international stabilisation force was deployed to help train Iraqi military personnel and develop the country's internal security institutions. Co-ordinated by US-led multinational force.
- Support to African Union in Darfur – Mission in Sudan (AMIS) 2005-2007.
- NATO no longer needed – an 'anachronism'.
- Undermines role of UN as primary world body for preventing/ending conflict.
- Dominated by US in terms of funding, troops and subsequent policy. Obama met Medvedev to discuss cuts in nuclear missile (July 09) arguably this is what matters not NATO.
- Continued widening of membership and disagreement over funding contributions (France & Germany) and troop deployment (eg Afghanistan) makes policy agreement more difficult.
- Afghanistan – Response to 9/11, 'war on terror'/Taliban/al-Qaeda. Aim to assist the Afghan authorities in providing security and stability. ISAF took over from US-led coalition in 2006. In 2008, there were 50,700 NATO troops from 41 countries. 2008 'worst year for violence for NATO'. 'Downward spiral' as Taliban has proved resilient. However, it is argued that Afghan economy has recovered and the country's infrastructure has improved. Obama's troop surge 2009 & 2010.
- NATO strength concerns Russia and it is argued that this has encouraged developments in arms technology (US missile defence system in Poland and Czech Republic); Russia "will think of retaliatory steps". Russia has resumed military flights off coast of Scotland and 'show of strength' in May Day parades (09). Russian fears of 'being surrounded' eg if Ukraine joins NATO.
- In 2008, Russian military involvement in Georgia (South Ossetia and Abkhazia) led to strongest condemnation from NATO but NATO has been unwilling to stop these territories from becoming 'independent' of Georgia.

- NATO ships active in Middle East (Gulf of Aden) to prevent piracy.
- Iran has tested Shahab missile system with range of 2000km (can reach Greece, etc.)
- Other relevant points.

MODERN STUDIES HIGHER
PAPER 2
2010

Question 1

Karen McDonald says, *"Year after year, male death rates are higher than female death rates for all causes and men have lower life expectancy across Scotland."*

Source C1(a) shows she is **incorrect** as far as male death rates are concerned as annually strokes kill more women.

But she is **correct** with regard to Source C1(b) as male life expectancy is lower than female life expectancy across Scotland.

Question 2

(a) Karen McDonald claims: *"Annually the number of males exceeding the recommended alcohol guidelines continues to increase."*
She is exaggerating because Source C2(a) shows the percentage of Scottish males exceeding recommended guidelines on alcohol intake is **falling**.

(b) William Walker claims that: *"In any event, more women now smoke than men in every age group."*
He is exaggerating as Source C2(b) shows that more men smoke in three of the six age groups eg 25-34 years age group male smokers 35% to female smokers 28%.

Question 3

William Walker says: *"Surveys show most men wanted Well Man Clinics open in the evenings and a majority were unhappy with the information they received."*
Source C3(b) shows William to be **correct** as most men (77%) would have liked to see Well Man Clinics open in the evening.
Source C3(a) shows that he is **incorrect** as most men (85%) were happy with the information they received from Well Man Clinics.

Note: When answering questions 1 and 3 candidates must quote fully from the sources and provide evidence to support and oppose the view.

Question 4

Credit will be given for:
A style appropriate to a report (sub-headings, chapters, etc) with:
- an introduction that indicates an awareness of the role to be adopted and makes a clear recommendation
- developed arguments in support of the recommendation
- identification of and comment on (rebuttal of) counter arguments
- provision and use of appropriate background knowledge
- an overall conclusion.

Arguments for the proposal may feature:
- male health/death rates/life expectancy worse
- relatively small investment with long-term financial savings
- men not making full use of traditional GP services and need additional help to change lifestyles
- gender equality legislation means men should not be treated less favourably for services than women.

Argument against the proposal may feature:
- WMC don't reach the type of men who most need to change their lifestyles
- waste of scarce resources/not value for money
- priority should be policies to reduce poverty and economic inequality not men's health
- not all men agree correct approach to improving men's health.

Credit will also be given for background knowledge which may be developed from the following statements:

Source A
- Numerous reports prove that the health of men in this country is worse than the health of women.
- …recent equality legislation eg Gender Equality Duty, Equality Bill 2008/09, etc.
- …on those issues particular only to males.
- …the many educational health campaigns being run by the Scottish Government.
- …wider approach to health care that looks at tackling the various causes of Scotland's poor health.

Source B
- …Scotland's abysmal health record.
- … "nanny state" approach.
- …the Scottish Government needs to address the underlying causes of social and economic inequality.
- …the link between poverty and poor health has been well documented.
- …other health education programmes.

Other background knowledge may include:
- Details of Well Man Clinics pilot or in Eng. 'Health of Men Initiative'.
- Reports on social/economic health inequalities.
- Scottish health problems eg the Big 3 killers.
- Scottish Government policies to combat health inequalities eg phasing out prescription charges, P1-P3 free school meals, etc.
- Scottish Government health promotion campaigns on healthy living, curbing alcohol sales, the smoking ban, etc.
- Knowledge of communities with particular health issues eg East End of Glasgow and links with joblessness.
- Other relevant points.

MODERN STUDIES HIGHER PAPER 1 2011

Section A – Political Issues in the United Kingdom

Study Theme 1A – Devolved Decision Making in Scotland

Question A1

"Pass" and better answers should feature developed, exemplified knowledge and understanding of:

Opportunities for MSPs to take part in the decision making process.
Extent of the influence of MSPs on decision making in the Scottish Government.
And
Balanced comment/analysis of the extent to which MSPs influence decision making in the Scottish Government.
Answers may refer to:

- Principles of Scottish Parliament include openness, responsiveness and accountability.
- Scottish Parliament electoral system means that it is unlikely that one party will dominate. Most likely scenario is coalition or minority government. Influence of individual MSPs is arguably greater.
- SNP minority Government. Must rely on support of other parties to pass legislation. Defeated over trams, minimum alcohol pricing and plans to replace Council Tax with Local Income Tax. Had to drop plans for a Referendum Bill. Past difficulties in passing Finance Bills (Budgets): Conservative MSPs able to secure a commitment to extra police officers, etc.
- Agreement in 2007 between SNP and Scottish Green Party to co-operate although in 2009 Budget was passed with support from all parties except Greens.
- First Minister's Question Time (214 oral questions/9,744 written questions answered in Chamber 2009-10). Possible for opposition to influence decision making but FM has backing of Civil Service that puts opposition at disadvantage. Alex Salmond regarded as strong FM but can be held to account eg apology over so-called loss of 'tartan tax' powers.
- Questions to Ministers.
- Committees. There are around fifteen committees. Some are mandatory eg Equal Opportunities and Public Petitions. Others are subject committees eg Education and Long Life Learning. Range and scope of committees huge with inquires in recent years on the Scottish economy, tourism and child poverty in Scotland.
- Most MSPs are members of at least one committee. Committees conduct inquires and produce reports. Scrutinise Government legislation and have power to alter bills. Committees can put forward their own proposals for new legislation in the form of committee bills.
- The Commission on Scottish Devolution (Calman Commission) was set up by opposition parties to review devolution in Scotland. SNP Government did not support motion to set up.
- Scottish Government does not require legislation to implement all policy eg abolition of prescription charges or bridge tolls.
- Impact of S.P. elections. SNP majority Government 2011.
- MSPs have right to introduce legislation (Member's Bill). Patrick Harvie's Bill (Offences (Aggravation by Prejudice

Act 2009)) was adopted by SG. However MacDonald's End of Life Assistance Bill, where MSPs had a free vote, was defeated.

- Other relevant points.

Study Theme 1B – Decision Making in Central Government

Question A2

"Pass" and better answers should feature developed, exemplified knowledge and understanding of:

Ways different groups outside Parliament seek to influence decision making in Central Government.
Extent of influence of different groups outside Parliament on decision making in Central Government.
And
Balanced comment/analysis on the view that some groups outside Parliament have more influence on decision making than others.
Answers may refer to:
- Use of the media campaigns, petitions, lobbying, rallies and demonstrations, publicity stunts eg those used by (New) Fathers 4 Justice campaign.
- Direct action eg fuel protests of 2000 and 2007; recent anti-capitalist protestors; student protestors.
- Backing of MPs by trade unions and private businesses.
- Use of internet including Facebook, Twitter and YouTube. MySociety on-line campaign played a part in ensuring MPs expenses would be released under FOI.
- Evidence to suggest numbers of PG and range of activities has risen in recent years.
- The influence of the media on decision making.
- Pressure groups extend opportunities for participation and provide channel of communication between government and people.
- Insider and outside groups. Insider groups have close links with government departments or other official bodies. They are trusted and negotiate quietly often out of sight so difficult to gauge their influence. Outsider groups which lack recognition seek to convert and mobilise public opinion using such tactics as demonstrations and rallies.
- Groups with larger memberships or more money, causes that are compatible with government views and or arise from specific circumstances (Snowdrop campaign) are more likely to be successful.
- Sectional/Interest exist to defend or promote interest of their members eg trade unions or National Farmers Union. Cause groups exist to promote a cause eg nuclear disarmament or the abolition of blood sports.
- Success of high profile Ghurka campaign led by Joanna Lumley and of trade unions campaign to prevent part-privatisation of Royal Mail. Success of others, such as Jamie Oliver's campaign to improve quality of food to school pupils, are more difficult to determine.
- Cash-for-influence affair (similar to MPs Cash for Questions affair in the 1990s).
- 1.7m people signed e-petition on Downing Street website in 2007. In 2009, government decided to scrap plans for a national road charge scheme.
- Failure to Save the Scottish Regiments campaign.
- Arguably, internet-based pressure convinced the UK Government to open up MPs expenses to public scrutiny.
- Influence of senior civil servants.
- References to influences on peers in the House of Lords.
- Other relevant points.

Study Theme 1C – Political Parties and their Policies (including the Scottish Dimension)

Question A3

"Pass" and better answers should feature developed, exemplified knowledge and understanding of:

The ways in which party leaders are elected.
The importance of the party leader in achieving electoral success.
And
Balanced comment/analysis on the view that the choice of party leader is crucial to electoral success.

With reference to at least two political parties, **answers may refer to:**

Conservatives
- Two stage election process since 1998: system established by William Hague. Stage 1 involves Conservative MPs voting in secret until two candidates left. Stage 2 involves party members in postal vote between two candidates (OMOV).
- Election is triggered by resignation of Party Leader or by 15% of Conservative MPs writing to Chairman of the 1922 Committee supporting a motion of no confidence in the leader.
- If leader gets simple majority of Parliamentary Party (51%+) then no election challenge can be made for twelve months. If leader loses vote of no confidence, leader resigns and cannot stand in the election which follows. David Cameron elected leader December 2005.
- Nominated for leadership passed to Chairman of 1922 Committee.
- Procedures for electing Scottish Conservative leader.

Labour
- When in opposition, leadership election is triggered by 12.5% of the parliamentary Labour Party.
- When in government, election requires two thirds support of party conference votes.
- Since 1993, leader chosen by electoral college comprising of three equal sections: Labour MPs and members of the EU parliament, constituency party members and trade unions affiliated to the Party.
- Election based on principle of One Member One Vote (OMOV).
- Within constituency section, every CLP has one vote which is given to the leadership candidate who wins ballot of individual members.
- Within the trade union section, every affiliated trade union is given a share of the overall trade union vote based on size of trade union membership. Every affiliated trade union hold a postal ballot of its members and its electoral college votes are divided between the candidates according to their share of the postal ballot.
- Procedures for electing Scottish Labour leader.

Liberal Democrats
- Any MP can stand provided they have backing of at least 7 colleagues and 200 party members from 20 different constituencies. Election by STV. All 73,000 party members entitled to vote.
- Nick Clegg narrowly elected leader October 2007.
- Procedures for electing Scottish Liberal Democrat leader.

Scottish National Party
- Leader and deputy leader elected by simple majority. Alex Salmond polled 75% of vote in September 2004 election (Nicola Sturgeon 54% of vote for deputy).
- Analysis of importance of party leader in achieving electoral success:

- Cameron is widely held to have improved Conservative fortunes. He has tried to embody the deeper changes the Conservatives have made to their policies and image; more inclusive and less 'nasty'.
- Apart from a brief 'Brown bounce' in September 2008 at the start of the economic crisis, Brown's leadership is widely seen to be a liability to Labour's electoral success. There have been frequent rumbling of a leadership challenge culminating in the 'coup that never was' in June 2009.
- Salmond is widely seen as an asset to the SNP. A shrewd politician who dominates the Scottish Parliament. The SNPs electoral fortune picked up after returned to the membership in 2004. In contrast, neither Iain Gray nor Tavish Scott have had much of an impact. Annabel Goldie has been a better performer on TV and in the Scottish Parliament but not enough to revive fortunes of Scottish Conservatives.

- Other relevant points.

Study Theme 1D – Electoral Systems, Voting and Political Attitudes

Question A4

"Pass" and better answers should feature developed, exemplified knowledge and understanding of:

The factors affecting voting behaviour.
The relative importance of different factors affecting voting behaviour.
And
Balance comment/analysis on the view that some of the factors affecting voting behaviour are more important than others.

Answers may refer to:
- A range of factors are said to affect voting behaviour including:
  - Media.
  - Social class.
  - Age.
  - Gender.
  - Residence.
  - Ethnicity.
  - Image of party leader.
  - Issues.

- Candidates who integrate factors will be credited highly. For example, social class and media can be seen as separate factors but they are related. Professional class voters may cross different newspapers, television and websites from lower class voters and are therefore exposed to a different set of media influences.

- Models of voting behaviour including social structures model and rational choice model. Debate as to extent to which rational choice model has taken social structures model. Some commentators (Sarlvik and Crewe) argue that absolute class voting and relative class voting have steadily declined and that 'issue voting' has become more important. Others (Heath) argue that although class voting has declined it remains the most important underlying factor affecting voting behaviour. The most recent studies (Manza, Hunt and Brooks) agree more with Heath.

- Tactical voting.
- Dealignment.
- Third party choices.
- Non-voting.

- Evidence of voting patterns from 2010 UK General Election (or other elections).

- Discussion of relative importance of different factors eg importance of Iraq War in relation to Muslim vote 2005, emphasis placed on successful media campaign by political parties, impact of 'economic crisis/recession', etc.

- Other relevant points.

Section B – Social Issues in the United Kingdom

Study Theme 2 – Wealth and Health Inequalities

Question B5

"Pass" and better answers should feature developed, exemplified knowledge and understanding of:

The link between poverty and health.
Other factors that may also affect health.
And
Balanced comment/analysis on the view that poverty is the most important factor that affects good health.

Answers may refer to:
- Health reports including 'Equally Well' (2008); annual 'Health in Scotland' reports; research from Glasgow Centre for Population Health; WHO Lenzie/Calton Report 2008, etc.
- Statistics in terms of mortality and morbidity. Scottish Government figures show that in 2007:
  - average life expectancy for males in Scotland was 74.9 but only 57.3 years in most deprived area. East Dunbartonshire was 78.0 years for males
  - under 75 deaths from heart disease and cancer were markedly higher in most deprived areas.
- Impact of low income:
  - welfare dependency
  - poor housing
  - run down local environment and effect on physical and mental health
  - Oxfam's 'FRED': Forgotten, Ripped off, Excluded, Debt.
- Harry Burns' research on 'biology of poverty'. Experience of being brought up in 'chaotic circumstances' has an effect on the body's immune system leading to a more unhealthy life, longer recovery from illnesses/operations and lower life expectancy.

- Other factors may include:
  - lifestyle choices (inc. smoking, alcohol, diet, drug misuse and exercise)
  - hereditary factors
  - gender
  - race
  - availability and uptake of preventative medical care
  - access to private medical acre.

- Candidates who avoid over simplification and acknowledge that certain health issues transcend class differences eg alcohol misuse or lack of exercise will be credited highly.

- Other relevant points.

Question B6

"Pass" and better answers should feature developed, exemplified knowledge and understanding of:

Government health and welfare provision.
The debate over government/individual responsibility for health and welfare.
And
Balanced comment on/analysis as to whether or not health and welfare provision should be the responsibility of government.

Answers may refer to:
- UK and Scottish Government health and welfare provision may include:
  - National Health Service
  - Benefits – JSA, State Retirement Pension, Pension Credit, Child Benefit, Income Support, Employment Support Allowance, tax credits, free   prescriptions in Scotland, etc.
- Founding principles of the Welfare State – universalism with flat-rate contributions (NI) giving 'cradle to grave' coverage.

- Debate over extent of government health and welfare provision. Individualism and collectivism. Individualists stress importance of self-reliance and need to avoid a 'dependency culture' whereas collectivists stress importance of fairness and equality in society.
- Labour's 'Third Way' – policy of 'welfare to work'. Welfare Reform Bill 2009 aims to further support people back into work as putting more responsibility on claimants to move towards work or lose benefit.
- Increased use of means testing welfare system against a background of rising costs.
- Impact of an ageing population. Future rises in ratio of dependents to workers.
- Widening of health and wealth gaps between most and least affluent.
- Strong public support for NHS. 2009 opinion poll in Guardian suggests public want NHS to be protected from future public expenditure cuts.
- SNP Scottish Government has been collectivist in approach eg free prescriptions and free school meals P1-3.
- Major political parties agree that health and welfare provisions is the responsibility of both the Government and the individual. The role of Government is to help the individual help themselves.
- 2009, Labour has proposed extending 'free' social care for the elderly in their own homes in England and Wales.
- Cameron's view on welfare – big government is wasteful and fails; talks of 'social entrepreneurs and community action'; proposed reforms to NHS in England and Wales; challenges to idea of 'Big Society'.

- Other relevant points.

Section C – International Issues

Study Theme 3A – The Republic of South Africa

Question C7

"Pass" and better answers should feature developed, exemplified knowledge and understanding of:

Government policies to reduce social and economic inequalities. Extent to which government policies have been effective in reducing social and economic inequalities.
And
Balanced comment/analysis of the effectiveness of government policies to reduce social and economic inequalities.

Answers may refer to:
- Black Economic Empowerment (BEE) is main growth strategy. Introduced in 2003 it also aims to ensure all South Africans have equality of opportunity. Operates through series of codes of practice (adopted 2007). Replaced GEAR (1996-2000) which aimed to develop SA economy through promotion of more open market, privatisation and increased foreign investment. This policy had only limited success.
- Accelerated and Shared Growth initiative aims to halve poverty and unemployment by 2014.

- Expanded Public Works Programme to create one million work opportunities by 2009.
- National Skills Fund widened to assist young, unemployed and lesser skilled.
- Increased in spending on education and health. Number of students in Higher education to 750,000. Most South Africans now live within 5km of health facility.
- Programmes to ensure everyone has access to drinkable water, sanitation and electricity.

- Inequalities within and between races in terms of housing, health, income, poverty, education, employment/ unemployment, crime and health.
- Gini co-efficient for South Africa has widened in recent years (0.6) with inequalities growing fastest amongst blacks (0.64).
- In 2007, 80% of people had electricity in home (58% 1996), 70% water in home (61%), 71% sanitation (50%).
- SA Government figures show 40% of people live in poverty – more than half surviving on less than one dollar a day. UN figure is higher with most being black.
- White unemployment is around 8% but Black unemployment may be as high as 50%.
- Increase in black middle class ('Black Diamonds') to 2.6m. Black representation reached 22% in top management in 2007.
- Decrease in income poverty for most South Africans but increase in levels of white South African poverty.
- Average white household salary 5.5 times the average black salary (2008) but difference falling.
- 2.3m new houses completed with 3.1m housing subsidises provided to improve housing.
- Government target of delivering 30% of agricultural land to black majority unlikely to be met as only 5% redistributed by 2007.
- SA described as "45/55" society – 45% in poverty and 55% not.
- Inequalities between provinces – Guateng wealthiest province, Eastern Cape poorest.
- Economic impact of 2010 World Cup.

- Other relevant points.

Study Theme 3B – The People's Republic of China

Question C8

"Pass" and better answers should feature developed, exemplified knowledge and understanding of:

Social and economic change.
Impact of social and economic change.
And
Balanced comment/analysis of the extent to which social and economic change has benefited the people of China.

Answers may refer to:
- Market economy has been steadily developing since early 1980s. Encouragement of individual initiatives and entrepreneurship.
- China joined World Trade Organisation in 2001. Third largest economy in world (US $4.32 trillion 2008).
- Introduction of Household Responsibility System. Today most farms operate as private businesses.
- Dismantling of work permit system (hukou).
- Foreign investment, encouragement of private business, changes to banking system.
- In 2009, Hu stated that China will continue to develop its 'socialist market economy' although US did not recognise China as a market economy at that time.
- Recession has seen government establish control over some privately owned businesses eg in airlines, steel and coal industry.

- Majority in China has benefited from social and economic reform but all have not benefited equally.
- Rise in average per capita income to $4644 (2009).
- Richest 10% of Chinese population account for 33.1% of consumption, poorest 10% only 1.8%.
- In 2009, 43m Chinese people below revised poverty line of 1,100 yuan per year but big decrease from 200m in poverty in 1978.
- A World Bank report 2006 stated income of bottom 10% of Chinese people had decreased by 2.4% in that year.
- Urban rural contrasts. Between 2005-07, one-third of rural households experienced poverty. Urban incomes growing at between 10-15% per year, far higher than rural incomes.
- Availability of private health care and private education.
- Environmental pollution and loss of land, housing, etc for some groups of people.
- Increase in corruption, crime, and other social ills of capitalist society.
- Hu's promotion of 'Harmonious Society' partly reflects CPC's concerns with growing inequality.
- Development of social security system.
- Increase in use of mobile phones and internet users. There is greater access to information on-line but many websites remain blocked eg Twitter.
- Constitution guarantees private property.
- 20m migrants have lost jobs as a result of the global economic crisis.
- Changes in some areas to one-child policy.
- Constitution guarantees religious freedom but little religious freedom in practice.
- Highest income groups in urban areas earn 5.6 times salary of lowest income groups.

- Other relevant points.

Study Theme 3C – The United States of America

Question C9

"Pass" and better answers should feature developed, exemplified knowledge and understanding of:

Government policies to reduce social and economic inequalities. Extent to which government policies have been effective in reducing social and economic inequalities.
And
Balanced comment/analysis of the effectiveness of government policies to reduce social and economic inequalities.

Answers may refer to:

- US Government/State welfare programmes. Most mainly funded by federal government but usually administered by state government includes:
  - Medicare, Medicaid and State Children's Health Insurance Program (covers children who do not qualify for Medicaid)
  - Temporary Assistance for Needy Families (TANF) introduced as part of Welfare Reform Act 1996 and ties welfare payments to the search for work. Limited to five years for cash support
  - Food stamps
  - Affirmative Action programmes as they apply today
- American Recovery and Reinvestment Act 2009 – economic stimulus package worth $787bn. $82bn of package is to provide for expansion of unemployment benefits, social welfare provision, education and health care.
- Some States have more generous programmes of welfare support than others.
- No Child Left Behind (NCLB) 2001 – aimed to improve performance in public schools to improve qualifications/ employability of all children. Backed with big increases in federal funding but on-going debate as to success.

- US has a rising Gini coefficient rating of over 0.4 one of the highest amongst developed nations.
- In 2007, Congressional Budget Office study found that incomes rose by 35% in some families affected by 1996 changes in US Government welfare to work programmes. On the other hand, many other families, many of which are black have experienced increased poverty.
- Race, gender and geographic inequalities in terms of housing, income, poverty rates, health, crime, education and employment/unemployment, etc.
- Success of minority groups and others – creation of Black middle class, Hispanic and Asian businesspeople, some Asian groups in terms of education, etc., do better than Whites.
- The debate over Affirmative Action.
- Prevailing individualist view within US society and that it is not government's responsibility to reduce social and economic inequality.
- Impact of Obama's proposed healthcare reforms which, if successful, would reduce the social inequality of access to healthcare.

- Other relevant points.

Study Theme 3D – The European Union

Question C10

"Pass" and better answers should feature developed, exemplified knowledge and understanding of:

The main social and economic policies of the EU and their agreed aims.
Social and economic policy on which there is disagreement within the EU.
And
Balanced comment/analysis of the extent of disagreement on social and economic policy among member states on the EU.

Answers may refer to:

- Enlargement – Seven potential new members to existing 27. Croatia likely to join 2011. Others, including Turkey which started negotiations for entry in 2005, will take longer. The Ukraine and Georgia have also been talked about as future members of the EU.
- Common Agricultural and Fisheries Policy. Disagreement over cost, implementation, success, etc.
- Monetary union – In 2009, 22 countries were using the euro with more to follow. Only the UK, Denmark and Sweden have not moved to the euro.
- EU Budget – 133.8bn euros in 2009. Most spent on agricultural subsidies and rural development (47% of total spend) and regional aid (32%).
- Working Time Directive and the opt-out. UK is continuing to resist pressure to end its opt-out from the maximum 48-hour working week.
- Lisbon Treaty/Reform Treaty – mainly political reform of EU but as new treaty amends Treaty on the European Union (Maastricht) and Treaty of Rome (established EC) credit. Includes new powers to EC, EP and European Court of Justice with regard to justice and home affairs.
- Disagreement between different political blocs (liberals, socialists, etc.) as well as between stages eg over immigration/free movement of labour.

- Enlargement debate. Supporters of further EU enlargement highlight the economic benefits of bigger EU market. The EU is now the single biggest market in the world. Opponents have concerns over impact of further enlargement in respect of cost and decision making.
- Disputes between member nations over CAP and CFP. Some countries such as France, Ireland and Greece do well from CAP. New EU members getting less from CAP than

older EU members. Supporters of CAP say it is vital to rural communities, others argue costs too much and benefits relatively few people. EU Commission aims to bring a reformed CFP into existence by 2013.
- UK (and other) rebate.
- 2008 accord struck on the detention and deportation of illegal immigrants after years of disagreement.
- Lisbon Treaty/Reform Treaty came into force 2009. Aims to streamline EU institutions to make EU operate more efficiently. Ireland, Denmark and the UK will have right to opt in our out of any new policies in the area of justice and home affairs. Poland may also eventually opt out from charter of Fundamental Rights.

- Other relevant points.

Study Theme 3E – The Politics of Development in Africa

Question C11

"Pass" and better answers should feature developed, exemplified knowledge and understanding of:

The importance of education and health care on development. Other factors that influence development.
And
Balanced comment/analysis of the importance of health and education overall in securing successful development in Africa.

*For this question, candidates must demonstrate specific knowledge of at **least one** African country.*

Answers may refer to:
- Extent of education/health provision in developing countries in Africa. May be taken from a variety of sources eg UN Development reports. Reference can be made to:
  - low levels of adult literacy
  - low level of school enrolment
  - high levels of illiteracy
  - low level of expenditure on health and education (public and private) in both actual and percentages terms
  - low life expectancy
  - infant/child mortality rates
  - other related measures of health and education development.

- Education and health are seen as fundamental to a country's economic and social development.
- Examples of improved education/health care and link to increase levels of development.
- The Millennium Development Goals (MDGs).

- Other relevant factors that influence development include:
  - good governance
  - terms of trade
  - conflict
  - debate
  - aid and international investment
  - types of levels of natural resources.

- Other relevant points.

Study Theme 3F – Global Security

Question C12

"Pass" and better answers should feature developed, exemplified knowledge and understanding of:

The ways the UN deals with threats to international peace and security.
The debate over reform on the UN.
And
Balanced comment/analysis of the view that the UN must reform to be more effective when dealing with threats to international peace and security.

Answers may refer to:
- In 2008, UN Secretary-General Ban Ki-moon outlined plans for reform of the UN. He sought to strengthen UN's capacity for preventative diplomacy as well as increase UN's ability to support peace efforts once conflict had ceased.
- There are fifteen of UN's Security Council, five of which are permanent – the P5 who have power of veto – with the other ten members elected.
- General Assembly Task Force on Security Council Reform encompasses a variety of proposals, such as eliminating the veto held by the five permanent members, and expansion of the Council.
- On-going discussions with regard to financial contributions/spending.
- Calls for the UN to have a force of its own.

- View that it is easier to be critical of the UN rather than see where it has been 'quietly successful' eg Cyprus, Kashmir, Liberia and the Democratic Republic of Congo. In 2009, the UN had 17 on-going peace missions around the world.
- Criticism of UN in respect of Bosnia, Rwanda, Somalia, Kosovo and Darfur.
- View that although UN's institutional arrangements are complex, the real problem for the UN is that its members are deeply divided about what they want from it.
- UN largely ignored by USA (and other countries) in respect of Iraq.
- North Korea and Iran's continued defiance of UN with regard to nuclear capability.
- Style of UN Security-General. Kofi Annan very high profile and wishing to be seen to be involved. Ban Ki-moon more low-key working hard in the background.
- Responses to terrorism – UN Global Counter = Terrorism Strategy.
- In 2001, UN Security Council authorised US to overthrow the Taliban in Afghanistan and for US and allies to set up the International Security Assistance Force (ISAF).

- Other relevant points.

MODERN STUDIES HIGHER
PAPER 2
2011

Question 1

Ken Dorward states, *"However, since 2007, the number of people on low incomes has risen while the relative value of the NMW in the UK is one of the lowest in the developed world."*
Source C1 shows he is **correct** as the number of people on low incomes has started to rise from 2007.
But he is **incorrect** with regard to Source C2 as the relative value of the NMW in the UK is not one of the lowest in the developed world. The UK lies fourth behind France, Australia and the Netherlands.

Question 2

Ken Dorward states, *"Few people believe that an £8 per hour NMW will push up wage rates in other areas of employment."*
Ken exaggerates because Source C3 shows 40% of people surveyed believe a higher NMW will push up wages in other areas of employment. This is highest percentage response.

Question 3

Christine Kelly states that, *"The UK now has very few households living in poverty compared to other European Union countries."*
Christine exaggerates because Source C4 shows UK is fourth highest in table just below Greece, Italy and Spain. UK is also above EU average.

Question 4

Christine Kelly states, *"Opinion surveys show that the public agree with the idea of a NMW but an £8 NMW but an £8 NMW would have a disastrous affect on a businesses such as hotels and restaurants where the majority of low paid workers are found."*
Source C3 shows Christine to be correct as 85% of people surveyed agreed with the idea of a NMW.
Source C5 shows that she is incorrect as only 12% of low paid workers are found in hotels and restaurants.

Note: When answering questions 1 and 4 candidates must quote fully from the sources and provide evidence to support and oppose the view.

Question 5

Decision Making Task or Report
- The report **must** feature background knowledge to pass
- Use must be made of all specified sources

A style appropriate to a report (sub-headings, chapters etc) with:
- an introduction that indicates an awareness of the role to be adopted and makes a clear recommendation
- developed arguments in support of the recommendation
- identification of and comment on (rebuttal of) counter arguments
- provision and use of appropriate background knowledge
- an overall conclusion.

Arguments for the proposal may feature:
- poverty levels rising; help meet poverty targets and end poverty wages
- reduce social inequalities – collectivist approach
- simplified tax and benefit system
- stimulate economy
- make work 'pay' and encourage workforce to become more skilled

Argument against the proposal may feature:
- harm economic recovery; hurt business relative to foreign competition

- unjustified: UK NMW relatively high
- individualist approach best way to tackle poverty and reduce inequality
- employees should be paid only what they are worth
- increase wages across employment levels

Credit will also be given for background knowledge which may be developed from the following statements:

Source A
- "...government...targets to reduce poverty..."
- "...a collectivist approach..."
- "...the social problems poverty creates..."
- "...extent to which society has become more divided has become all too clear."
- "complicated and costly process of means-tested benefits could be scrapped..."
- "Many politicians believe the NMW is too low."

Source B
- "...worst recession in fifty years..."
- "The rates of pay for the NMW currently ensure there are no poverty wages in this country."
- "...range of benefits and government programmes to support the poorest groups in society."
- "...dependency culture..."
- "multinational companies..."
- "...UK unemployment rates are historically high..."

Other background knowledge may include:
- Number and types of workers currently benefiting from NMW
- Year NMW introduced/details of NMW 16-17 or 18-20
- The individualist/collectivist debate
- Consequences of widening social and economic inequalities
- Extension of adult NMW to 21 year olds 2010

Section A – Political Issues in the United Kingdom

Study Theme 1A: Devolved Decision Making in Scotland

Question A1

"Pass" and better answers should feature developed, exemplified knowledge and understanding of:

The roles and functions of local government in Scotland.
Conflict (and co-operation) between local government and the Scottish Government.
And
Balanced comment/analysis of the view that in carrying out its functions local government has come into conflict with the Scottish Government.

Answers may refer to:

- Provides opportunity for people to take part in local decision making which in theory makes for better governance.
- Mandatory, discretionary and permissive functions of local government. Local authorities also play a regulatory role eg granting licences and an advocacy role in promoting the interests of local communities.
- 32 unitary authorities (29 mainland and 3 island councils).
- Collaboration between local government and voluntary sector in delivering services.
- Scottish Parliament is law-making body for devolved issues. It can pass laws setting out the powers and duties of local authorities.
- Councils receive around 80% of funding from Scottish Government (Aggregate External Finance which includes non-domestic rates). Most other finance comes from Council Tax, rents and charges for services.
- STV electoral system means Scottish councils are often run by a coalition which includes representatives from the same party as the Scottish Government. Local government offers a pathway to the Scottish Parliament. SNP has largest number of councillors (263) and formed Scottish Government for first time in 2007.
- 'Concordat' (Single Outcome Agreements) between Scottish Government and local authorities from 2007-11. Councils given increased budgets and less ring-fencing in return for Council Tax freeze.
- Demands for end to Council Tax rise freeze. Threat of cut to local authority budgets if CT freeze not maintained.
- PFI/Scottish Futures Trust. Opposed in principle and in practice by many councillors.
- Recommendations of Independent Budget Review (Beveridge) of public spending in Scotland. Reduction in Scotland's budget by as much as £42bn over 16 years. Recommendations included a fall in public sector employment by as many as 60,000 by 2014-15 and public sector pay freezes. Glasgow Council claim cuts in grants will 'kill the city'.
- On-going speculation with regard to reducing number of councils or the centralisation of delivery of some council services eg education, fire service.
- Spat over severe weather school closures – councils unhappy at SG interference in local decision making.
- Disagreement over Edinburgh trams project, Trump golf course in Aberdeenshire, etc.

- Introduction of CFE exemplifies inherent tension between national government introducing national initiative but relying on 32 LAs to implement. Position of East Renfrewshire Council.
- Other relevant points.

Study Theme 1B: Decision Making in Central Government

Question A2

"Pass" and better answers should feature developed, exemplified knowledge and understanding of:

The powers of the Prime Minister.
The opportunities afforded Parliament to exercise control over the powers of the PM.
And
Balanced comment/analysis on the view that Parliament is effective in controlling the powers of the Prime Minister.

Answers may refer to:

- Prime Minister has power to:
  - Appoint, reshuffle or dismiss ministers
  - to set government agenda eg calling and chairing Cabinet meetings; appointing members of Cabinet committees and deciding terms of reference
  - patronage: appoint ambassadors, top civil servants, judges, etc., and create peers/give out honours, use of the whip
  - control of Cabinet Office
  - increase in power of Prime Minister's Office
  - dissolve Parliament.

- Prime Minister is public face of government/national leader and no longer seen as 'first among equals'.
- In media age personality of PM has become more important. Argument that collective government has been replaced by 'presidential government' eg Blair's 'sofa government'.
- General Elections increasingly seen as battle between PM and Leader of Opposition eg series of national debates before 2010 Election.

- Limits to powers:
  - appointments require some need for political balance and administrative competence eg Blair's retention of Brown as Chancellor or Clegg as Deputy PM.
  - PM is leader of party and government but must retain support of both to continue. Support is conditional and based on performance and that PM seen best as chair rather than a president.
  - answerable to Parliament eg Prime Minister's Question Time.
  - rebellions (proposed EU referendum Nov 2011) and votes of no confidence.
  - limitations imposed by a coalition government eg compromise politics or in appointments eg Vince Cable's criticisms of his Government's policies.
  - role of House of Lords.
  - Fixed Term Parliament Act (2011) provides for General Elections every five years.

- Other relevant points.

Study Theme 1C: Political Parties and their Policies (including the Scottish Dimension)

Question A3

"Pass" and better answers should feature developed, exemplified knowledge and understanding of:

The policies of the main political parties.
Extent to which the policies of the main parties differ.
And
Balanced comment/analysis on the view that there are few policy differences between the main political parties.

Answers may refer to:

Differences/similarities in policy can be within or between parties in Scotland or the UK. Candidates may refer to law and order, taxation, education and Europe as specified in the arrangements, or any of the points below.

Conservatives

- Development of the 'Big Society'; planned reduction in welfare role of State.
- Ensure economic stability; reduce budget deficit quickly.
- Abolish Income Tax rate of 50%.
- Limit immigration.
- Scrapping of ID Cards.
- Match Labour's health and aid spending promises: managerial reforms and opening up NHS to new, independent and voluntary sector providers.
- Opt out from Charter of Fundamental Rights.
- Contracting out of police services.

Labour

- Support for further devolved decision making in Scotland (as Lib Dems).
- Reduce Government spending in the longer term to protect jobs and services.
- Continue to develop public services; commitment to more apprenticeships.
- Support increases in the National Minimum Wage.
- Extension to paternity leave; support for greater childcare provision.
- Referendum on the voting system: change to a wholly elected House of Lords.
- Health: opposition to UK Government's proposals for NHS in England/Wales.

Liberal Democrats

- Commitment to reduce taxation for lowest earners; close tax loopholes for wealthy.
- Higher priority for environmental policy.
- No replacement of Trident nuclear weapons system.
- Scrapping of ID Cards.
- Shake up of education system in England and Wales.
- Constitutional change including reform of voting system (AV referendum lost), an elected House of Lords and a Freedom Bill.
- Differences within Liberal Democrats over tuition fees.
- Banking reform.

Scottish National Party

- Independence for Scotland.
- Commitment to support the scrapping of ID cards and Trident nuclear system.
- Protection of Scottish jobs with a focus on economic recovery especially in renewables; commitment to additional modern apprenticeships.
- Maintain public spending in the short-term to ensure economic recovery ('More Nats, Less cuts').
- Scrap the House of Lords and the Scotland Office; reduce Quango numbers.
- More funding/powers to the Scottish Parliament and greater fiscal autonomy.
- Protect free personal care for the elderly.
- Fuel duty regulator.
- Single police force for Scotland.
- Since 2010, Conservative and Liberal Democrat coalition in Westminster. In Scotland parties are in opposition.
- Labour was in coalition with the Liberal Democrats in the Scottish Parliament 1999-2007.
- Differences within and between parties emerged with regard to the 2011 AV referendum. 68% to 32% voted no to AV.

- Credit similarities and differences in policy within and between parties in relation to the 2011 Scottish Parliament elections.

- Other relevant points.

Study Theme 1D – Electoral Systems, Voting and Political Attitudes

Question A4

"Pass" and better answers should feature developed, exemplified knowledge and understanding of:

Influence of the media as a factor affecting voting behaviour. Other factors that affect voting behaviour.
And
Balanced comment/analysis on the extent to which the media is the most important factor affecting voting behaviour.

Answers may refer to:

- Most people get their political news from television, which by law must remain neutral.
- 2010 saw the first live leaders debates. Huge viewing figures; "Cleggmania". But the leaders debates did not translate into large scale support for the Liberal Democrats.
- The press can be as partisan as it wishes; an issue with the popular press.
- There is little hard evidence that newspapers themselves directly influence voters; big decline in newspaper sales in recent years.
- Some voters may choose a newspaper that supports their political outlook or they mainly read stories that agree with their politics or they skip the political pages altogether.
- Political parties still court partisan press support. The Sun and Daily Mail are seen to be barometers of the critical "floating voter" opinion.
- Newspapers court the social class, age, gender and race of their readers by building their "political" message around what they believe their readers want to read.
- In 2010, 'The Sun' urged voters not to back Labour. This does not mean that it was "The Sun Wot Won It". Public opinion had already turned against Labour.
- The Sun's defection though, demoralised the Labour campaign and this may have impacted on voting behaviour.
- In 2007 Scottish election, tabloid papers went against the SNP but the SNP still won.
- In 2011 The Scottish Sun supported SNP, boosting the party's morale.
- Parties are increasingly using social media to connect with and motivate both core and floating voters.
- SNP has been particularly astute in its use of twitter, Facebook and "virals".
- Credit highly candidates who discuss other factors eg class, leadership but relate these to media, rather than as an isolated or "shopping list" factor.
- Social class is still important. But this is related to media usage as working class are more likely to read tabloids.
- Leadership is a critical factor, but this too is related to the leader's ability to manage the media, eg Gordon Brown's poor media showing via Youtube, Sky "bigotgate", Iain Gray's Subway episode. These can be compared with Alex Salmond's showing on Question Time before 2011 Scottish elections.
- Role of the media in exposing sleaze/scandal eg MPs expenses. However, media becoming the news (NotW) and weakening their influence. Murdoch's performance at CMS select committee.
- Other influences that affect voting behaviour include social class, age, gender, ethnicity, etc.

- Other relevant points.

Section B – Social Issues in the United Kingdom

Study Theme 2 – Wealth and Health Inequalities in the United Kingdom

Question B5

"Pass" and better answers should feature developed, exemplified knowledge and understanding of:

The aims of the UK Welfare State.
The extent to which the UK's Welfare State meets its aims.
And
Balanced comment/analysis on the view that the Welfare State continues to meet its aims.

Answers may refer to:

- Welfare State – a system of social protection with the state taking the lead role in caring from 'cradle to grave'.
- Designed to tackle the 'Five Giant Evils' (squalor, ignorance, want, idleness and disease) as identified by Beveridge in 1942. Post-war, resulted in an expansion of health (creation of NHS 1948) and education services, introduction of greater social security coverage and measures to improve housing.
- Developed with the principles of universal provision and flat rate contributions.
- Health:
  - Aims to be universal, comprehensive, free at 'point of need', high quality
  - Increases in life expectancy, lower death rates, wide range of high quality services, etc.
  - waiting lists and waiting times, hospital infections, staff shortages, food quality, etc.
- Education:
  - Provision from nursery to university level; specialised provision.
  - Rises in educational results, increased numbers at university, record investment.
  - international comparisons, numbers leaving school with no qualifications, shortages of staff and educational materials, cuts in education spending, etc.
- Social Security
  - wide range of benefits to many groups inc. elderly, children, those with disabilities, etc.
  - benefit levels are low, 'dependency culture', accessibility/complexity of benefits, etc.
- Housing:
  - local authority council housing provision, specialised provision eg sheltered housing, etc.
  - shortage/quality of available council housing, homelessness, etc.
- Other eg Children's Services inc. fostering, adoption, etc.
- Increased real term spending on welfare provision in last 10 years. Cut backs since 2010.
- Charges for some NHS services eg prescriptions (free Scotland 2011), eye and dental charges.
- UK welfare state described as a 'liberal model'. Clear distinction between the 'deserving' and 'undeserving poor'.
- Other countries have more generous welfare state systems.
- Right wing/individualist view that welfare state is expensive, unsustainable, encourages dependency and delivers poor support; left-wing collectivist view that welfare state is integral to decent society, reduces poverty and reduces inequality.
- Blair's 'Third Way' and Cameron's 'Big Society'.
- Differences between Scotland, England and Wales eg prescriptions, care for elderly or tuition fees.
- Coalition plans to 'remodel' the WS by ending 'dependency' or universality of Child Benefit. Attempts to 'encourage' disabled and long-term unemployed on Incapacity Benefit back to work.
- Coalition Government claim they meet fundamental principles of welfare state as they support those "genuinely in need". Beveridge did not intend to support those wilfully choosing a life of welfare dependency.
- Credit candidates who take a view and argue coherently that the aims of the WS are no longer relevant for the 21st Century
- Other relevant points.

Question B6

"Pass" and better answers should feature developed, exemplified knowledge and understanding of:

Government policies to reduce gender **or** race inequalities.
Extent of gender **or** race inequalities in the UK.
And
Balanced comment/analysis on the view that Government has failed to reduce gender **or** race inequalities in the UK.

Answers may refer to:

- Equal Pay Act; Sex Discrimination Act; Equality Act; The Commission for Equality and Human Rights; Gender Equality Duty Code of Practice; Women's Enterprise Task Force; Equality Act 2010.
- Work and Families Act extended the right to request flexible working; extended further 2009.
- CTC and Working Tax Credit. Affordable child care ('wraparound childcare') as crucial to narrowing the wage gap.
- MW has disproportionately benefited women and minorities. Maternity and paternity leave.

- Gender pay gap: UK women in full time work earn 10% less per hour (2010). Higher for part-time work.
- Women make up 60% of the university population; success of women in reaching senior posts varies from place to place. 'Glass ceiling' only cracked, not broken.
- Women make up only 22% of MPs; only 12% of directors in FTSE 100 firms are women despite accounting for over 46% of the labour force.
- Sex and Power Report 2008.

- Pay gap has narrowed in some areas.
- Graduate unemployment is higher for males.
- In 2010, 20% of married women out-earn their partners; around 19% earn the same.
- Four in five paid carers are women. The care sector's poor pay contributes greatly to the gender pay gap.

- Race Relations Acts.
- Tackling Race Inequality 2010.
- Black Pupils Achievement Programme/Aiming High Strategy, REACH and Ethnic Minority Employment Task Force.
- One Scotland.
- Unemployment higher amongst minority groups; far higher for 18-24 year olds; employment rates for ethnic minority groups lower but gap narrowing.
- Growing evidence of a 'race pay gap'.
- Very few board members are from ethnic minority groups 'Race for Opportunity Report.
- Stephen Lawrence verdict evidence that UK society has moved on from 1993 when Met police accepted it was "institutionally racist".
- Women from Black Caribbean, Pakistani and Bangladeshi groups most likely to face a higher risk of unemployment, lower pay and have fewer prospects for promotion. EOC's 'Moving On Up? The Way Forward' report 2007.

- 'Glass door'.
- Credit references to health policies and success or otherwise in reducing gender or race inequalities.

- Other relevant points.

Section C – International Issues

Study Theme 3A – The Republic of South Africa

Question C7

"Pass" and better answers should feature developed, exemplified knowledge and understanding of:

Main features of the South African political system/extent of ANC support.
The debate surrounding the ANC and their use of power.
And
Balanced comment/analysis of the view that the political strength of the ANC does not threaten democracy.

Answers may refer to:
- SA is a constitutional democracy with a three-tier system of government.
- Federal state with nine provincial governments.
- Bicameral parliament elected every five years, comprising the 400 seat National Assembly and the 90-seat National Council of Provinces.
- Local government elected for 4 years; 284 metropolitan, district and local municipalities.
- Party List electoral system.
- 13 political groups represented in National Assembly.
- Constitution guarantees many rights including property rights and education; two-thirds of members of Parliament and at least 6 provinces need to support change to Constitution.

- 2009 was 4th General Election since Apartheid era, each won by ANC with large majorities. ANC obtained 65.9% of votes to National Assembly (264/400 seats). ANC also won 8/10 of the provincial legislatures. NA has 90 members. ANC 62 with DA 13 and COPE 8 – the remanding 8 seats shared between 5 other different parties.
- ANC won a majority in most of the councils. The DA won the largest share of votes in the City of Cape Town but no majority. The IFP won the majority in KwaZulu-Natal Province.
- 15 different political parties represented in Parliament.
- 26 parties contested all municipal or local elections in 2006. ANC won 66.36% nationally, with DA 14.8% and IFP 8%.

- The constitution provides for freedom of the press, and this is generally respected. Laws, regulation and political control of media content are considered to be moderate and there is little evidence of repressive measures against journalists.
- Newspapers and magazines publish reports and comments critical of the government, although the state-owned SABC is less likely to criticise.
- Hallmarks of democracy present: stable economy, survival of the constitution despite ANCs dominance in the chamber after 2004 election, many opposition parties and pressure groups, legal system pursuing corruption.
- Prevention and Combating of Corrupt Activties Act of 2004 a person in a position of authority who knows or reasonably suspects another person of fraud must report it to the police.
- Various corruption scandals that have affected the ANC. COPE made corruption an issue in 2009 election. Zuma has had corruption charges levelled against him on more than one occasion.

- Several respected organisations including SA trade unions have said that fraud and corruption could compromise the rule of law. Helen Zille said in Oct. 2009 that the ruling party is subverting the constitution and judiciary.
- Deputy President Motlanthe stated in Aug. 2010 that fight against crime and corruption must first start with ANC; speech came after two major corruption scandals involving high profile ANC figures.
- In 2008, Mbeki disbanded the Scorpions a combined police and prosecution unit that investigated corruption. Mbeki also dismissed independent head of the National Prosecution Authority.
- Motlanthe says he stands by rule of law and independent judiciary. Independent and well respected lawyer Edwin Cameron appointed to Constitutional Court.
- 2010 Media Bill (Protection of Information Bill) seen as threat to press freedom.
- Effectiveness of opposition parties – arguably still somewhat fragmented and divided. Some evidence ANC tolerates opposition rather than respects.
- Concerns about ANC intolerance towards media opposition.
- Criticism by Archbishop Tutu that Zuma's ANC is "worse that apartheid rulers". Claims ANC has lost touch with its roots and its leaders corrupted by power.

- Other relevant points.

Study Theme 3B –The People's Republic of China

Question C8

"Pass" and better answers should feature developed, exemplified knowledge and understanding of:

China's political and human rights record.
Recent moves towards democracy and better human rights.
And
Balanced comment/analysis on the view that democracy has been extended and human rights improved.

Answers may refer to:
- Political rights – despite a Constitution guaranteeing freedoms and fundamental rights, the same Constitution describes the 'democratic dictatorship' led by the working class. Role of the People's Liberation Army; registering of all organisations which may oppose the CPC single-party state.
- Evidence of 'a lack of human rights': right to a fair trial, religious freedom, One-child policy, media control, lack of fair trial, death penalty, laogai, Falun Gong, Tibet, women's rights.
- Media – 1982 constitution guaranteed freedom of speech – however, 'subversion of state power' clause used against critics. Government runs main News Agency; forbids ideas on Tibetan independence; forbids any challenge to CPC power; blocks the internet.
- Legal – double appeals process in place since 2007. Saw 15% overturn of death penalty in first half of 2008. 30% fewer death penalties in 2007 compared to 2006. 55 crimes eligible for death penalty, down from 68 in 2010. Representation now allowed in courts.
- Olympics 2008 – International criticism of human rights lead to increasing dialogue and acceptance of improvements to work towards. Deported foreign protesters; 'Protest parks' allowed, but of 77 applications, 74 withdrawn, 2 suspended and 1 vetoed.
- Incidents of foreign reporters complaining of restrictions, intimidation and violence, however, also publicised that relations were more positive and improving.

- Religion – 1982 Constitution allows the right of freedom of belief, however CPC members must be atheist. CPC tries to control not only content but leadership eg latest Catholic leader appointed by state, not the Pope in 2007. Restrictions to practices on Tibetan Buddhism.
- Hong Kong – 'One country – two systems' with greater political freedom.
- Little tolerance of dissent groups, although criticism of corrupt local officials accepted. Liu Xiaobo author of Charter 08 jailed for 11 years on subversion charges. Liu Xiaobo awarded Noble Peace Prize. Mrs Liu under house arrest.
- Number of strikes, demonstrations and riots has grown 22% annually indicating rising discontent amongst 'losers' in the economic transformation eg expropriation of farmland and real-estate development in urban areas, food and environmental scandals suggest potential challenge to regime. However, not too likely as more 'winners' and those with political status believing that CPC strategies are necessary in the long term.
- Village elections since 1998 and now in about 650,000 villages; 75% of population.
- In 2008 Shenzhen 'highest GDP area – selected to elect government officials at district level'; 70% to be directly elected, however, selected from a pre-approved list.
- CPC argue welfare of all should always be above rights of the individual. A strong and stable authority must regulate potential conflicts. They claim social breakdown in the West is a result of excessive individual freedom.
- 'One-size-fits-all' definition of human rights should not apply internationally.

- Other relevant points.

Study Theme 3C – The United States of America

Question C9

"Pass" and better answers should feature developed, exemplified knowledge and understanding of:

The powers of the US President.
The ways in which Congress can act to check the powers of the President.
And
Balanced comment/analysis on the extent to which Congress acts as an effective check on the powers of the President. Credit references to Supreme Court if linked to President and Congress.

Answers may refer to:
Presidential powers include:
- Chief Executive, Commander in Chief of the Armed Forces (power to wage war); responsible for treaty negotiation.
- Chief formulator of public policy – legislation dealt with by Congress drafted by Executive branch.
- Power of appointment: 6,000 new federal positions from top government officials. Nominates judges but requires Senate confirmation. Appoints top officials for federal agencies.
- Executive Orders do not require Congressional approval eg Bush Federal aid after Hurricane Katrina. Obama: softened ban on gays in military; regulation of heat-trapping gases; bi-partisan budget commission under his authority. Attempted closure of Guantanamo Bay; removal of barriers for stem cell research, etc.
- Department of Homeland Security and Patriot Act designed to give more power to President; a legacy of 9/11.
- Presidential vetoes (regular and pocket) or threat of veto.
- President can grant reprieves and pardons without confirmation – GW Bush commuted or rescinded 200 convictions; Obama had granted 68 to midway 2010.

- Executive privilege – established by precedent not the constitution. Nixon and Clinton famously denied this privilege.
- 'Extraordinary powers' – Bush administration in 'War on Terror'.
- Presidential interventions.

Limits to presidential powers include:
- Congress sets the budget of the Executive, so a check on Presidential power.
- 2/3 majority can overturn a Presidential veto, except a pocket veto.
- Process and timings of elections. Mid-term elections (2010) altered the balance of power and thus support in the House of Representatives; Republicans control lower house
- Senate advice and consent required for the appointment of Cabinet members, ambassadors, judges and other senior executive officers. Obama had to threaten Senate with recess appointments in Feb. 2010.
- Congress has sole power to pass Constitutional amendments.
- House impeaches with a simple majority and Senate convicts with a 2/3 majority.
- Senate has to ratify treaties.
- Health reform – a major election policy for Obama has 'ping ponged' between the Executive and Congress since his election, passed March 2010; difficulties with 'American Jobs Act'. But White House Chief of Staff Daley looking at range of executive orders and directives as "White House can't wait on Congress". Supreme Court involved and will rule in July 2012 if President Obama's healthcare reforms are constitutional.
- Congress held up closure of Guantanamo; refusal to resettle detainees in US.
- Credit references to Supreme Court where links are made between President, Congress and Supreme Court.

- Other relevant points.

Study Theme 3D – The European Union

Question C10

"Pass" and better answers should feature developed, exemplified knowledge and understanding of:

The powers of the European Parliament.
The powers of the other EU institutions.
And
Balanced comment/analysis of the importance of the decision making powers of the European Parliament within the European Union.

Answers may refer to:
- EP has 732 elected members; one of three key decision-making institutions.
- EP has say in 80% policy areas including agriculture and home affairs issue. Role in legislative process expanded over time as the scope of EU policy has grown.
- Amsterdam Treaty – EP and European Council sharing legislative power and must both approve a Commission proposal to become law. Lisbon Treaty enhancing EP role even further as its role of forming a bicameral legislature alongside the European Council becomes the ordinary procedure.
- Votes on Commission's programme and monitors management of EU policies through oral and written questions.
- Role in EU's legislative and budgetary processes and general supervision of the Council and the European Commission.

- Budget – EP and Council have joint powers.
- Has right to dismiss entire Commission through a vote of censure. May also reject newly-proposed Commission and individual members – 2004 threatened veto to Commission headed by Jose Barroso who had to change proposed team to ensure EP approval.
- EP must approve new member states and all agreements entered into with non-member countries – eg trade agreements.
- Co-decision does not cover all aspects of EU policy eg tax and foreign affairs.
- Increasing checks and balance role, and increased forum for debate on international issues, although foreign policy rests with member states.
- The Council is the main EU decision making body, comprising Ministers from national governments.
- Discusses proposals put forward by the Commission, amends if necessary, but is then passed to the EP in its role within a bicameral procedure.
- As decisions by the Council are subject to qualified majority voting (QMV) rather than unanimity (increases speed and efficiency in decision making) the Parliament's role seen as an increasingly important democratic counterweight.
- The Commission initiates legislation. It is the executive and guarantor of treaties.
- Post Lisbon Treaty the future of the new constitutional arrangements in doubt as France and Netherlands and Ireland initially voted NO, adding to the claim that there is no public interest or engagement in the EU Parliament.
- Strain on the EU with regard to debt and future of the EU; national governments having to address not EU Parliament.

- Other relevant points.

Study Theme 3E – The Politics of Development in Africa

Question C11

"Pass" and better answers should feature developed, exemplified knowledge and understanding of:

Foreign aid in its various forms.
Factors that limit the effectiveness of foreign aid.
And
Balanced comment/analysis of the effectiveness of foreign aid in promoting development.

Candidates must demonstrate specific knowledge of at least one African country.

Answers may refer to:
- The impact of aid from international organisations, national governments (eg DIFD) and NGOs (eg Oxfam, Save the Children, etc).
- Work of UN agencies (WHO, UNESCO, FAO, UNICEF) and programmes (WFP, etc.)
- Candidates may adopt a case study approach eg Malawi irrigation scheme in Thyolo area giving small plots of land and advice to farmers. However, government withdrawal of financial support for these extension services in the expectation of private sector investment, which has not happened. Action Aid blames World Bank with its fixation on agriculture for economic growth and not food supply.
- Debate that aid is needed to promote development/save lives and those who see aid as encouraging dependency.
- More than 10 years since Millennium Development Goals. Progress towards all goals – extensive poverty and hunger reduction, improvements in primary education enrolment and child mortality rates, reductions in HIV/AIDS rates, etc, but (sub-Saharan) Africa remains poorest continent.

- The impact of debt/debt cancellation. Annually, debt repayments exceed aid received. Structural adjustment programmes made things worse – only 5 countries cleared debt under HIPC (Heavily Indebted Poor Country) initiative.
- View the 'free trade' not 'free aid' will do more to promote development; break cycle of dependency.
- Terms of world trade including fluctuations affecting cash crops. Dumping of subsidised farm products on local markets. Import tariffs and restrictions.
- Impact of 'recession'.
- War. In 2010, 13 countries affected. Obstacles to development – destruction, death, scorched earth tactics, disruption to food supplies, financial costs, etc.
- Corruption within governments: Zimbabwe – Mugabe, Liberia – Charles Taylor.
- Agriculture progress report of World Bank questioned by Action Aid with special reference to Uganda where agriculture extension programmes were stopped. Other reports question the sustainability of Uganda's Poverty Eradication Action Plan.
- Divided views within the UN on the way forward and failure of many members to reach the 0.7% of GNP to UN for development programmes.
- Effect of natural disasters.

- Other relevant points.

Study Theme 3F – Global Security

Question C12

"Pass" and better answers should feature developed, exemplified knowledge and understanding of:

The changing role of NATO and the threat from international terrorism.
Other threats to international peace and security.
And
Balanced comment/analysis of the view that NATO now sees international terrorism as the main threat to global peace and security.

Answers may refer to:
- Founded 1949, NATO retains traditional collective security role but also aims to promote democracy and encourage co-operation in order to avoid conflict.
- 28 countries are members of NATO; increase in partnerships with other countries across world eg Russia (NATO-Russia Council).
- New 'Strategic Concept' adopted at Lisbon Summit 2010 aims to develop NATO's capabilities to meet new emerging threats eg international terrorism, cyber attacks or nuclear proliferation.
- 9/11/'War on Terror':
  - National security focus/increased restrictive legislation eg in UK – control orders, USA – Patriot Act, also increased airport security, bio-passports, surveillance operations, etc.
  - Afghanistan: International response. NATO entered Afghanistan 2001. Aim to defeat Taleban/destroy al-Qaeda (capture Bin Laden). NATO (ISAF) looking to hand control of security to Afghan forces in 2014.
- Anti-terrorism operations – 'Operation Active Endeavour' in the Mediterranean/Arabian Gulf. Also, looking to prevent illegal movement of people, arms or drugs that help finance terrorism.
- Recognition of the threat that terrorism poses – former UN Secretary General claimed terrorism a threat to international peace and security; high on UN agenda (UN Security Council meeting on international peace and security addressed by H. Clinton, 2010).

- Terrorism is not new but has taken on a new international dimension post 9/11. al Qaeda in particular has stated aims and targets of significantly wider focus.
- al-Qaeda global terrorist organisation. Numerous attacks around world eg London and Mumbai. Difficult to counter as groups operate separately from one another. Shift in location of al-Qaeda to Yemen. Oct. 2010 explosives found on cargo plane heading for USA but with stop over in UK.
- Importance of peacekeeping role: eg Kosovo (KFOR) in support of the United Nations and in support of peacekeepers elsewhere in the world.

Other threats to global peace and security which may be referred to include:

- Nuclear proliferation – Iran's defiance of UN in its attempts to enrich uranium.
- Middle East – Israel/Palestine or continued instability in Iraq.
- North/South Korea – clashes threatened to escalate Nov. 2010.
- India/Pakistan; instability caused by al Qaeda/Taleban and war in Afghanistan.
- Expansion of NATO – seen as threat to Russia – Georgia/Abkhazia/S. Ossetia/Chechyna.
- Instability in Tunisia and Egypt ('Arab Spring'). NATO's involvement in Libya (providing air and logistical support in arming the Libyan rebels) and not in Syria.
- Global drug trade – seen as major issue for both UN and NATO.
- Competition over resources – eg oil and water.

- Other relevant points.

MODERN STUDIES HIGHER PAPER 2 2012

Question 1

Stephen Morris states, *"Statistics show Scottish universities have, on average, a minority of students with parents from a working-class background, with Edinburgh and Glasgow universities having the lowest figures"*.

Source C1 shows he is **correct** as only a minority of university students are from working-class background eg Scotland average 28.2%.

But he is **incorrect** as St Andrews has the lowest intake of students from a non-professional background.

Question 2

Stephen Morris states, *"Currently, the professions are completely dominated by those who have been privately educated at fee-paying schools."*

This is exaggerated as Source C2 shows that the senior positions are not completely dominated by those privately educated eg only MPs 35% privately educated.

Question 3

Gillian Gilbert states that, *"Research shows that a majority of young people believe better advice and information would be most likely to help them enter a professional career."*

This is exaggerated as Source C3 shows that more young people believe more financial support (57%) is the best way to encourage young people into a professional career.

Question 4

Gillian Gilbert states, *"Although around a third of students from working-class backgrounds study subjects such as law or biological science, it would be better to encourage young people into skilled trades where wages are higher than professional salaries."*

Source C4 shows Gillian Gilbert to be **correct** when she states, *"Although around a third of students from a working-class backgrounds study subjects such as law or biological science…"* C4 shows that around a third of students from a working-class background do study biological science (33.8%) or law (34.1%).

But **incorrect** when she states, *"…it would be better to encourage young people into skilled trades where wages are higher than professional salaries"*. C5 shows that wages in skilled trades are not higher than professional salaries.

Question 5

Decision Making Exercise

Arguments for the proposal may include:
- lack of social mobility/continued class divide
- positive discrimination worked well for other groups
- wider benefits of less divided society
- economic benefits of proposals
- collectivist arguments.

Arguments against the proposal may include:
- unfairness of retaining 33% of university places for students from working-class backgrounds
- patronising to students from working-class backgrounds
- additional support already exists to overcome inequalities
- emphasis should be on boosting status of vocational training
- individualist arguments.

Background information that may be developed from the Sources may include:

- development of any of the arguments from above or
- support in schools to raise attainment
- initiatives to promote university education
- changes in employment patterns/unemployment statistics
- legislation/impact of legislation to eliminate discrimination.

Other possible background knowledge:

- implications of the Equality Act 2010
- impact of government spending cuts
- funding and the welfare state
- evidence of a range of social/economic inequalities in Scotland.
- Relevant comment on success/failure of broader affirmative action programmes in countries such as USA or South Africa.

Reports failing to include background knowledge will not pass.

MODERN STUDIES HIGHER PAPER 1 2013

Section A – Political Issues in the United Kingdom

Study Theme 1A: Devolved Decision Making in Scotland

Question A1

'Pass' and better answers should feature developed, exemplified knowledge and understanding of:

- The powers/additional powers of the Scottish Parliament
- Limitations to the powers of the Scottish Parliament

And

balanced comment/analysis of the view that with additional powers the Scottish Parliament can better deliver Scottish solutions to Scottish problems.

Answers may refer to:

- The devolved powers of the Scottish Parliament include:
- Health
- Education
- Local Government
- Law
- Social Work and Housing
- Economic Development and Transport
- The Environment; Agriculture, Forestry and Fishing; Sport and the Arts
- Additional powers contained in the Scotland Act 2012 (from 2015) and closely follows the final recommendations of the review of devolution (Calman Commission):
- Scottish income tax rate to raise around 35% of revenue/Scotland-specific taxes (including stamp duty and landfill taxes)
- Airguns legislation; drink driving legislation; national speed limits
- Scottish Parliament will be able to borrow more money
- Scottish Parliament will be able to issue bonds to access cash from capital markets
- Implications of the 2014 referendum on independence
- But UK Parliament controls (reserved powers):
- Most taxes and benefits
- Employment
- Constitutional arrangements including Acts of Parliament to grant further powers or independence to Scotland
- Examples of the Scottish Parliament delivering Scottish solutions to Scottish problems:
- Smoking ban in enclosed public spaces (before rest of UK)
- Free personal care for elderly
- Abolition of prescription charges
- No university tuition fees
- Issue for nationalists is that SP lacks power to fully deliver Scottish solutions to Scottish problems.
- Debate over 'Devo Max' – greater fiscal autonomy but stopping short of independence.
- Legislation on sectarianism, minimum pricing and compensation for asbestos sufferers.
- Other relevant points.

Study Theme 1B: Decision Making in Central Government

Question A2

'Pass' and better answers should feature developed, exemplified knowledge and understanding of:

- The role of the Cabinet in the UK Central Government
- Other influences on decision making in UK Central Government

And

balanced comment/analysis of the extent of the importance of the Cabinet in decision making in UK Central Government.

Answers may refer to:

- Cabinet is the collective decision making body in UK political system. Meets every Tuesday.
- Cabinet composed of most senior members of ruling party/parties. Around 22 paid Ministers form the Cabinet plus several select others.
- Prime Ministers seek to have a confident, united Cabinet.
- Parliamentary majority normally means that the Executive, with assistance from Parliamentary whips, can have legislation passed by Parliament.
- Prime Ministers and the Government cannot rule effectively without high degree of Cabinet unanimity eg Brown said to be undermined by lack of Cabinet support. Cameron needs degree of consensus with Clegg and Lib Dems.
- Prime Minister selects Cabinet and can re-shuffle.
- Prime Minister uses powers of patronage to secure Cabinet compliance.
- Prime Minister can use collective responsibility to neutralise Cabinet members.
- "Dominance of PM "first among equals"
- Role of the media and election campaigns have heightened the "Presidential" nature of modern politics.
- Tony Blair relied on "sofa government"; SPADS (special advisers) and inner Cabinet ignoring Cabinet on key decisions.
- David Cameron is not as in control as previous Prime Ministers, with Lib Dem Cabinet Ministers in Cabinet eg Vince Cable Sky comments and comments on Cameron's immigration proposals.
- Cabinet resignations sapped the morale and confidence of Brown.
- Parliament can defeat the Executive; both the Commons eg detention without trial and the House of Lords (ID cards) have defeated Government (inc. Executive) in recent times; HoL defeated Government on benefit reforms several times.
- The importance of the Cabinet decision making process depends upon the specific nature and composition of the Government. The Con/Lib Dem Cabinet has to be more collegiate given the nature of coalition government.
- Other relevant points

Study Theme 1C: Political Parties and their Policies (including the Scottish Dimension)

Question A3

Conservative Party/Scottish Conservative Party

- Traditionally policy making decided by leadership.
- Party leadership given great freedom to decide policy as events dictate.
- National Conservative Convention and Conservative Political Forum allow party members to have input into policy but they remain advisory.
- Conservative backbench 1922 Committee is sometimes referred to as "the men in grey suits". They do not make decisions but the party leader takes great stock of their views.
- Party policy is essentially "top down".
- Party conference is deferential towards the party leadership.
- Divisions within Scottish Conservatives; Ruth Davidson did not win a majority of first preference votes in leadership election.

Labour Party/Scottish Labour Party

- Labour Party consists of Constituency Labour Parties, affiliated trade unions, socialist societies and the Co-operative Party with which it has an electoral agreement.

- Labour Party members tend to be more "ideological" than Conservatives and seek a greater input into party policy.
- Policy in the Labour Party is made through a process called Partnership in Power (PiP) which is designed to involve all party stakeholders (inc. ordinary party members). PiP does this through a rolling programme of policy development and a year-round dialogue between the party and government. Development of policy is carried out by six policy commissions.
- Members who are elected to parliamentary positions take part in the Parliamentary Labour Party (PLP).
- Party's decision-making bodies at a national level formally include the National Executive Committee (NEC), Labour Party Conference and National Policy Forum (NPF) although in practice the parliamentary leadership has the final say on policy.
- The Labour Party Constitution states that Party policies making up the Labour Party programme should be approved by the Conference, subject to receiving two thirds support. The election manifesto, which consists of policies from the programme, has to be agreed between the parliamentary leadership and the NEC.
- Leadership/NEC proposes programme and conference votes to support/reject programme with CLPs, affiliated organisations and trade unions having weighting according to number of members.

Liberal Democrats/Scottish Liberal Democrats

- Policy making body is the Federal Conference. Twice a year, in spring and autumn, elected representatives from the Liberal Democrat constituency parties assemble at the party conference to establish federal party policy. Representatives from every local party, organised around parliamentary constituencies, are elected to attend federal conference.
- Conference decides policy matters on national and 'English' issues; separate Scottish Liberal Democrat Party makes policy decisions on Scottish issues.
- Every two years, conference representatives elect a Federal Policy Committee (FPC) which is responsible for the production of the policy papers that are debated at Conference, and is responsible for election manifestos. Party members discuss policy papers in local and regional meetings, and their representatives then debate and vote on policy motions and papers at Conference. Conference also debates motions submitted by local parties and conference representatives.
- Clegg's position within coalition government as Deputy Prime Minister.

Scottish National Party

- Alex Salmond dominates the SNP. SNP included 'Alex Salmond for First Minister' on 2011 regional list ballot papers. Personality seen as SNP's greatest asset.
- Members can submit motions on policy and national strategy to be discussed by the party at national level.
- Local branches are drawn together to form a Constituency Association (CA). Branches and CAs send representatives to the two national bodies that agree the policies of the Party.
- The National Council and Annual National Conference. Annual Conference is the supreme governing body of the Party and elects the National Executive Committee, the leadership of the Party, which deals with the day-to-day running of its affairs.
- SNP Annual National conferences have, like other major party conferences, become less of a policy making body as the party has become a party of Government.
- Other relevant points.

Study Theme 1D: Electorial Systems, Voting and Political Attitudes

Question A4

Answers may refer to:

- AMS used to elect MSPs to the Scottish Parliament since 1999. Electors have two votes – one for constituency MSP and one for list MSP. In the constituency vote candidate with most votes wins. Second vote for a party in a region which is used to make the overall result in region broadly proportional.
- FPTP used to elect MPs at Westminster. Highest number of votes in constituency becomes MP; party with most MPs most likely to form government.
- Claimed that AMS provides better representation because:
  - has features of a PR system ie overall result is closer to way in which electorate voted
  - there has been greater representation of minority parties (Greens and in the past Socialists) and independents
  - notionally easier to elect women and people from minority ethnic backgrounds under AMS
  - AMS retains direct constituency/MSP link but can sometimes lead to 'turf wars' between list and constituency MSPs and arguably can confuse voters
  - Most likely result is a coalition (Labour/Lib. Dem 1999-2007) or minority government (SNP 2007-2011). Coalitions allow greater representation in government and minority government requires consensus in order to pass legislation/approve budget. Ironically (and who hasn't said this to their Higher class) AMS delivered majority SNP Scottish Govt. in 2011, whereas FPTP led to Con./Lib. Dem coalition in 2010. AMS can also be seen as 'undemocratic' as no-one voted for coalition or compromise politics
  - Some commentators feel that AMS leads to Scottish voters being 'over-represented' with 8 MSPs for each voter. Questions over the efficiency of this 'representation'

- Claimed that FPTP provides fairer representation as:
  - retains direct representative-constituent link
  - normally produces decisive electoral result. 2010 produced Con/Lib. Dem coalition; some evidence that coalitions may be more likely in the future
  - view that FPTP notionally provides for more stable, effective government and therefore better representation
  - But notionally harder for smaller parties to gain representation but first Green MP elected 2010 under FPTP, independents in earlier elections and the BNP had 28 councillors before 2010 (after 2010 English local elections)
- Referendum 2011 on introduction of AV for UK Parliament elections as a result of the perceived unfairness of FPTP.
- In 2010, few women MPs only 143 (21.5%) but 2% rise from 2005.
- Other relevant points.

Section B – Social Issues in the United Kingdom

Study Theme 2: Wealth and Health Inequalities in the United Kingdom

Question B5

'Pass' and better answers should feature developed, exemplified knowledge and understanding of:
- Lifestyle choices and their impact on good health
- Other factors that affect good health

And

balanced comment on/analysis of the view that individual lifestyle choices are the main factor preventing good health.

Answers may refer to:
- Positive lifestyle choices.
- Poor lifestyle choices inc. smoking, alcohol, diet, drug misuse and failure to exercise.
- Equally Well Report 2008/Review 2010.
- Scottish Parliament Health Inequalities Cross-Party group.
- Other reports, statistical information, etc.
- Other factors may include:
  - impact of poverty/deprivation
  - 'biology of poverty'
  - hereditary factors
  - gender
  - race
  - availability and uptake of preventative medical care
  - access to private medical care
  - age
- Credit highly candidates who avoid over simplification and acknowledge that certain health issues transcend class differences eg alcohol misuse or lack of exercise.
- Other relevant points.

Question B6

'Pass' and better answers should feature developed, exemplified knowledge and understanding of:
- Government policies to reduce poverty
- Impact of government policies on those in poverty

And

balance comment/analysis on the view that government policies have reduced poverty in the UK.

Answers may refer to:
- Wide range of Welfare State provision including State benefits, healthcare, education, housing and personal/children's social services.
- Debate over access, quality and extent of State support including means-testing of Child Benefit, tightening of benefit rules, etc.
- Proposed changes to welfare including the introduction of the Universal Credit, cap on benefit limits, 'bedroom tax', etc.
- References to official reports and statistics eg poverty levels among pensioners and children, unemployment statistics, statistics on inequalities by socioeconomic group, gender, race, etc. Stats may cover income, wealth, education and health outcomes, etc.
- Equalities legislation including Equality Act 2012 and impact.
- Credit references/comment on Scottish government policies eg end of prescription charges, free personal care for the elderly, etc.
- Poverty reduction targets (children, fuel poverty) set by previous Labour government will not be met. Conservatives looking to change way in which poverty measured ('non-income indicators of poverty'). IEA argues UK's poverty reduction strategy 'fundamentally flawed' and that new approach is needed.
- Official figures for 2011 found 18% of children (2.3m) lived in households classed as below poverty line a drop of 2% or 300,000 children from year before. Numbers in severe poverty also fell. Child poverty groups claim figure is higher, nearer 4m or more than 1 in 4 of all children. CPAG claims figure will rise in future.
- UK's Gini co-efficient is rising and higher than any point in last thirty years. OECD claims in equality rising faster in UK than any other rich nation.

- The poorest 10% of population have, on average, seen a fall in their real incomes after deducting housing costs; the richest 10% have seen bigger proportional rises in their income than any other group.
- Taxation has a smaller income redistributing effect than in the past.
- Studies argue that social mobility is falling as inequalities widen.
- Other relevant points.

Section C – International Issues

Study Theme 3A: The Republic of South Africa

Question C7

'Pass' and better answers should feature developed, exemplified knowledge and understanding of:
- South African government policies to reduce social and economic inequalities
- Impact of government policies

And

balanced comment/analysis of extent to which South African government policies have reduced social and economic inequalities.

Answers may refer to:
- Black Economic Empowerment (BEE) introduced in 2003. Operates through series of codes of practice. Broad-Based Black Economic Empowerment (B-BEE) from 2007.
- Affirmative Action policies aim to ensure all South Africans have equality of opportunity.
- Accelerated and Shared Growth initiative aims to halve poverty and unemployment by 2014.
- Expanded Public Works Programme (phase 2) aims to create 2m jobs and to halve unemployment.
- National Skills Fund widened to assist young, unemployed and lesser skilled.
- Spending on education and health (17% and 11% respectively of national budget).
- Programmes to ensure everyone has access to drinkable water, sanitation and electricity.
- Expanded social assistance and other grants by the Department of Social Development have greatly improved the lives of millions of beneficiaries (est. 12.4m 2011).
- BEE, arguably, helped only a minority of Black South Africans. B-BEE aims to distribute wealth across broader spectrum of society.
- Inequalities within and between races in terms of housing, health, income, poverty, education, employment/unemployment, crime and health.
- Gini co-efficient for South Africa has widened in recent years with inequalities growing fastest amongst blacks (0.57).
- SA Constitution's Bill of Rights provides everyone the right "to have access to housing, health care services, sufficient food and water and social security."
- Figures show 40% of people live in poverty. UN figure is higher with most being black. However, poverty levels overall have fallen.
- In 2010, white unemployment was around 5% but Black unemployment was 30% (but may be as high as 40%).
- Increase in black middle class ('Black Diamonds') to 2.6m.
- Decrease in income poverty for most S. Africans but increase in levels of white S. African poverty to around 10%.
- Average white household salary 7.7 times the average of black salary (2008) but difference falling.
- 2.3m new houses completed with 3.1m housing subsidies provided to improve housing.

- Government target of delivering 30% of agricultural land to black majority unlikely to be met. Zuma conceded "Willing buyer, willing seller" poicy had "not yielded desired result".
- SA described as "45/55" society – 45% in poverty and 55% not.
- Debate over success of Affirmative Action policies.
- Disappointment expressed by Desmond Tutu over progress of ANC. He claimed ANC is "worse than the apartheid government".
- Other relevant points.

Study Theme 3B: The People's Republic of China

Question C8

'Pass' and better answers should feature developed, exemplified knowledge and understanding of:
- Chinese government policies to reduce social and economic inequalities
- Impact of government policies

And

balanced comment/analysis of the extent to which Chinese government policies have reduced social and economic inequalities.

Answers may refer to:
- 12th five-year plan (from 2011) will see $1.5 trillion invested by state in seven strategic industries in next five years.
- Policies aimed at lifting incomes include the abolition of agricultural tax, new central and local government mandates to fund nine years of free education, improved health care and the construction of low-income housing.
- Majority in China has benefited from social and economic reform but all have not benefited equally.
- Gini co-efficient has grown in recent years to 0.47 (2010). A figure above 0.4 is regarded as an indicator of extreme levels of inequality.
- Rise in average per capita income to $4644 (2009). Officially wealthiest 10% of population earn 23 times that of the poorest 10%. However, some commentators claim true figure is much higher.
- Richest 10% of Chinese population account for 33.1% of consumption, poorest 10% only 1.8%.
- In 2009, 43m Chinese people below revised poverty line of 1,100 yuan per year but big decrease from 200m in poverty in 1978.
- Urban rural contrasts. In 2010, China's urban per capita annual income of about US $2,965 was three times that of rural residents (US $935). The gap is much more extreme in larger, wealthier cities such as Beijing ($9,085 in 2008) and Shanghai ($10,529 in 2008). 50% of Chinese live in rural areas.
- Increased availability of private health care and private education.
- Environmental pollution and loss of land, housing, etc., for some groups of people.
- Denial of access to health care, education and pensions to an estimated 150m migrant workers.
- Increase in corruption, crime, and other social ills in capitalist society.
- Hu's promotion of 'Harmonious Society' partly reflects CPC's concerns with growing inequality.
- Development of social security system.
- Increase in use of mobile phones and internet users. There is greater access to information on-line but many websites remain blocked eg Twitter.
- Constitution guarantees private property.
- Changes in some areas to One-child policy.
- Constitution guarantees religious freedom but little religious freedom in practice.

- Protests against rising unemployment, corruption, pollution, loss of land/housing, etc.
- Other relevant points.

Study Theme 3C: The United States of America

Question C9

'Pass' and better answers should feature developed, exemplified knowledge and understanding of:
- Ethnic minority participation in elections
- The importance of ethnicity as a factor influencing the outcome of elections

And

balanced comment/analysis of the extent to which ethnic minorities influence the outcome of elections in the USA.

Answers may refer to:
- Minorities make up 30%+ of US population and climbing; for presidential election, minority voters often concentrated in key 'swing states' giving disproportionate influence in those states eg California, Texas, New York and Florida.
- Blacks 12% US population; Hispanics 14%+; Asians 5%. Growing importance of Hispanic vote in closely divided states of Colorado, New Mexico, California, Arizona & Nevada in relation to presidential electoral college votes.
- Minority groups are less likely to register or to vote in elections but gap is closing. Hispanics made up 10% total vote 2012. Impact in 'swing states' of Colorado and Nevada.
- As many as 14m minorities are illegal and are not allowed to vote.
- Influence of Black Caucus and Hispanic Caucus.
- Most Blacks and Hispanics vote Democratic 2012 – 93% Blacks voted for Obama, 71% Hispanics. 60% Whites overall voted for Romney.
- White and Asian voters more mixed; Whites marginally favoured Republicans in 2008 and 2012.
- Greater representation of minority groups within Democrat Party at all levels.
- Other factors affecting voting in the US include:
  - Wealthier people of whatever ethnic minority more likely to favour Republicans; poorest more likely to vote Democrat (if they do vote)
  - issue voting inc. the economy/ unemployment, Obama's healthcare proposals, etc.
  - image of candidate Obama and McCain (age, experience); Obama and Romney (experience, background)
  - regionality North East/West traditionally more democratic and liberal; South and Mid-West Republican and socially conservative
  - gender
  - traditionally Democrats more interventionist; Republicans much less so.

Study Theme 3D: The European Union

Question C10

'Pass' and better answers should feature developed, exemplified knowledge and understanding of:
- The main social and economic issues within the EU
- Issues on which there is disagreement amongst EU member countries

And

balanced comment/analysis of the extent to which there is disagreement over social and economic issues within the EU.

Answers may refer to:
- Enlargement – Seven potential new members to existing 27. Croatia set to join 2013. Others, including Turkey will take longer. The Ukraine and Georgia have also been talked about as future members of the EU.
- Common Agricultural and Fisheries Policy – disagreement over cost, implementation, success, etc. Major changes to the CFP planned for 2013.
- Monetary union – In 2011, 17 EU member countries use the euro with more to follow. Only the UK, Denmark and Sweden have resisted any moves to the euro.
- EU budgets. 129bn euros in 2012. Biggest areas of expenditure are sustainable growth (inc. employment) and preservation and management of natural resources (inc. agricultural and rural development).
- Working Time Directive and the opt-out. UK is continuing to resist pressure to end its opt-out from the maximum 48-hour working week.
- Lisbon Treaty/Reform Treaty – mainly political reform of EU but as new treaty amends Treaty on the European Union (Maastricht) and Treaty of Rome (established EC) credit. Includes new powers to EC, EP and European Court of Justice with regard to justice and home affairs.
- Enlargement debate. Supporters of further EU enlargement highlight the economic benefits of bigger EU market. The EU is now the single biggest market in the world. Opponents have concerns over the impact of further enlargement in respect of cost and decision making.
- Disputes between member nations over CAP and CFP. Some countries such as France, Ireland and Greece do well from CAP. New EU members getting less from CAP than older EU members. Supporters of CAP say it is vital to rural communities, critics argue CAP costs too much and benefits relatively few people. EU Commission aims to bring a reformed CFP into existence by 2013. On-going discussions to further reform CAP.
- UK (and others) rebate.
- 2008 accord struck on the detention and deportation of illegal immigrants after years of disagreement.
- Lisbon Treaty/Reform Treaty came into force 2009. Aims to streamline EU institutions to make EU operate more efficiently. Ireland, Denmark and the UK will have right to opt in or out of any new policies in the area of justice and home affairs. Other members also have opt-outs.
- Economic crisis – disagreement over extent of support for euro/countries on brink of default eg Greece. Cameron's use of the veto over treaty change (Dec. 2011).
- Disagreement between different political blocs (liberals, socialists, etc.) as well as between states eg over immigration/free movement of labour.
- Other relevant points.

Study Theme 3E: The Politics of Development in Africa

Question C11

'Pass' and better answers should feature developed, exemplified knowledge and understanding of:
- Conflict as a factor limiting development in African countries
- Other factors which limit development

And

balanced comment/analysis of the view that conflict is the main reason for lack of development in African countries.

Answers may refer to:
- Credit highly candidates who integrate the various factors affecting development. Also, credit candidates who acknowledge that development is taking place at different rates across the continent.
- There have been numerous civil wars and conflicts across Africa. 15 African countries were involved in war or were experiencing post-war conflict and tension in 2011.

- In last 20 years, majority of deaths in world from internal or external conflict were in Africa.
- There have been over 9m refugees and internally displaced people in Africa since 2000.
- In addition to the human cost, there are economic, strategic and environmental costs associated with conflict. For example, the Democratic Republic of the Congo, has suffered more than a decade of civil war that, besides causing the deaths of about 4 million people, has cost it £9bn, or 29% of its gross domestic product, according to Oxfam. Eritrea, Burundi and Rwanda are among the other worst hit countries.
- In 2007, Oxfam report claimed that conflict had cost the African continent $150bn between 1990-2005 or the equivalent to all the foreign aid received over the same period.
- In 2011, leaders of the g7+ stated that to achieve the MDGs they need to focus on political settlements, security, justice and economic growth.
- Increased role of African Union (AU) in promoting peace and security across continent.
- According to the UN, free from conflict, a number of African countries have achieved growth rates and development achievements comparable to the most successful emerging economies around the world.
- World Bank report of 2011 recommended that aid should have a greater focus on building stable government than on health and education.
- GDP grew 6% across Africa in 2011.
- Other factors that influence development include:
  - extent of education and health care provision; battle against AIDS and malaria being won; more children are going to school
  - good governance
  - terms of trade
  - debt
  - aid and international investment
  - types and levels of natural resources
  - Other relevant points.

Study Theme 3F: Global Security

Question C12

'Pass' and better answers should feature developed, exemplified knowledge and understanding of:
- Ways in which the UN may respond to threats to peace and security
- Impact of UN responses on threats to peace and security

And

balanced comment on the effectiveness of the UN in dealing with threats to international peace and security.

Answers may refer to:
- The General Assembly of the UN is the main deliberative organ of the UN and is composed of representatives of all member states. The work of the UN derives largely from mandates given by the General Assembly. A revision of the General Assembly is currently taking place to enhance its role, authority, effectiveness and efficiency.
- The Security Council has primary responsibility, under the UN Charter, for the maintenance of international peace and security. Reform of the Security Council is under consideration.
- Functions and powers of Security Council include: maintain peace and security (conflict prevention); investigate disputes and recommend methods of resolving disputes (peace-making); controlling armaments in areas of conflict and/or calling on members to apply economic sanctions and/or to take military action against an aggressor (peace enforcement/peace-building).

- While decisions about establishing, maintaining or expanding peacekeeping operation are taken by the Security Council, the financing of UN peacekeeping operations is the collective responsibility of all UN member states. UN budget for peacekeeping in 2010-11 was $7.83bn. The US provided 27.14% of the UN's peacekeeping budget 2011-12.
- UN's democracy agenda (UNDEF). Established to support democracy; assistance given in wide range of countries including Afghanistan, Bosnia and Palestinian territories.
- View that it is easier to be critical of the UN rather than see where it has been 'quietly successful' eg Cyprus, Kashmir, Liberia and the Democratic Republic of Congo
- UN's view that its' peacekeeping missions are vital (peacekeeping supports a peace process; it is not a substitute), effective (with the proper mandate) and efficient and cost-effective.
- In 2011, there were 16 on-going UN peacekeeping missions around the world.
- Criticism of UN in respect of Bosnia, Rwanda, Somalia. Kosovo and Darfur.
- View that although UN's institutional arrangements are complex the real problem for the UN is that its members are deeply divided about what they want from it.
- Veto by P5 in UN Security Council has been block on UN taking effective action particularly by US in Middle East/Israel and Russia in Chechyna. US/UK criticism of China/Russia veto in response to Syrian government and internal unrest.
- UN largely ignored by USA (and other countries) in respect of Iraq.
- N. Korea and Iran's continued defiance of UN with regard to nuclear capability.
- Style of UN Secretary-General. Kofi Annan very high profile and wishing to be seen to be involved. Ban Ki-moon more low-key working hard in the background.
- Responses to terrorism – UN Global Counter-Terrorism Strategy.
- In 2001, UN Security Council authorised US to overthrow the Taleban in Afghanistan and for US and allies to set up the International Security Assistance Force (ISAF).
- UN backing for enforced no-fly zone (enforced by NATO war planes) which began process of Gaddafi's removal. View that the UN can have more immediate success when it works with an organisation such as NATO which has the military strength and/or a more robust mandate.
- There are an average of 50 conflicts in the world in any given year.
- Other relevant points.

MODERN STUDIES HIGHER
PAPER 2
2013

Question 1

Source A, Carrie Brody says, *"Currently, Scotland has the highest daily rate of smoking in the European Union"*.

Source C1 shows she is exaggerating as Scotland does **not** have the highest rate of smoking in the table of EU countries.

Question 2

Source A, Carrie Brody says, *"Deaths linked to smoking are highest in the most deprived parts of Scotland with around half of the people in the poorest social groups continuing to smoke"*.

Carrie Brody is **correct** as C2 shows deaths linked to smoking are highest in the most deprived parts of Scotland.

But she is **incorrect** as C3 shows less than a third of social groups C2, D and E continue to smoke.

Question 3

Source B, Nick Matheson claims that, *"Evidence suggests that those under the age of 20 are the age group most likely to smoke"*.

Source C4 shows that smoking rates are consistently **higher** in all other age groups except over 60+ years.

Question 4

Source B, Nick Matheson says, *"Surveys show that most people do not support an extension to the ban on smoking in public places but instead think year-on-year price rises are the best way to reduce smoking"*.

Source C5 shows he is **incorrect** as the public **do** support an extension to the ban on smoking in public places as 75% agree.

But Source C5 shows he is **correct** as he claims year-on-year price rises are seen as the best way to reduce smoking and this is highest in the survey (55%).

Question 5

DECISION MAKING EXERCISE

An introduction that indicates an awareness of the role to be adopted and makes a clear recommendation developed arguments in support of the recommendation identification of and comment on (rebuttal of) counter arguments provision and use of appropriate background knowledge an overall conclusion will be credited.

Arguments for the proposal may feature:
- Will make smoking more difficult and this will reduce smoking rates
- Health risks of smoking; cost to State
- Risk from second-hand smoke
- Role of legislation in driving health improvement

Arguments against the proposal may feature:
- Scottish Government has more pressing economic problems
- Attack on civil liberties

- Cost and unenforceability of PASS
- Wrong approach

Background knowledge may be developed from the following statements:

Source A
"Public health campaigns…"
"Legislation regulating the availability and advertising of tobacco"
"Treating illnesses associated with smoking…"
"In other parts of the world legislation to further restrict smoking has already proved successful…"
"…collective action…"

Source B
"…there are many more pressing social problems Scottish politicians need to tackle."
"…like many other lifestyle choices…"
"Individuals and not the State should decide the way in which adults in this country live their lives."
"There is already a huge range of health promoting initiatives in this country."
"…new ways to reduce smoking…"
"The Scottish Government would do better to tackle the causes of poor health, such as poverty…"

Other background knowledge may include:
Existing smoking legislation
Government campaigns to encourage people to stop smoking
Healthy eating initiatives
Minimum pricing of alcohol
'Shettleston man'
Harry Burns' 'biology of poverty'

MODERN STUDIES HIGHER
PAPER 1
2014

Question A1

Study theme 1A: Devolved Decision Making in Scotland

> **'Pass' and better answers should feature developed, exemplified knowledge and understanding of:**
>
> • Opportunities for MSPs to hold the Scottish government to account
> • Effectiveness of MSPs in holding the Scottish government to account
>
> **And** balanced comment on/analysis of the extent to which MSPs are effective in holding the Scottish government to account.

Answers may refer to:

- Key principles of Scottish Parliament include accountability, openness, participation and equal opportunities.
- Questions (oral and written) to Ministers/First Minister's Questions.
- Debates.
- Committees/Enquires.
- Voting.
- Examples of the above with reference to powers of Scottish Parliament including health, education, transport, justice, etc, and the additional powers included in the Scotland Act 2012.
- Since 2011 SNP majority government- in practice harder for opposition parties to oppose. Credit also references to when SNP was minority government (2007-2011) and had to build consensus with regard to the Budget or law making.
- Alex Salmond stated soon after the election in 2011 that SNP aimed to 'govern with consensus'.
- SNP dominate committee chairs but try to achieve consensus in decision making.
- Legislative Consent Motions (Sewel motions).
- Other relevant points.

Question A2

Study Theme 1B: Decision Making in Central Government

> **'Pass' and better answers should feature developed, exemplified knowledge and understanding of:**
>
> • Groups and methods used that influence decision making
> • Extent of influence of different pressure groups
>
> **And** balanced comment on/analysis of the effectiveness of pressure groups in influencing decision making in Central Government.

Answers may refer to:

- Insider and outside groups. Insider groups have close links with government departments or other official bodies. They are trusted and negotiate quietly often out of sight so difficult to gauge their influence. Outsider groups which lack recognition seek to convert and mobilise public opinion using such tactics as demonstrations and rallies.
- Cause/Interest groups.
- Use of media campaigns, petitions, lobbying, rallies and demonstrations, publicity stunts, etc.
- Direct action.

- Backing of MPs by trade unions and private businesses.
- Sectional/Interest exist to defend or promote interest of their members eg trade unions or National Farmers Union. Cause groups exist to promote a cause eg nuclear disarmament or the abolition of blood sports.
- Groups with larger memberships or more money, causes that are compatible with government views and or arise from specific circumstances are more likely to be successful.
- Examples of successful action include Ghurkhas winning right to settle in UK. Also: 'pasty tax' U-turn (VAT extension applied also to static caravan) after protest from bakers and caravanning enthusiasts; petrol duty freeze July 2012 after campaign by road users.
- Examples of failed pressure group activity eg those opposing army cuts or extension of wind farms.
- Credit references where candidates appreciate differences in aspirations within coalition government and this provides greater opportunities for groups outside parliament to apply pressure.
- Other relevant points.

Question A3.

Study theme 1C: Political Parties and their Policies (inc. the Scottish Dimension).

> **'Pass' and better answers should feature developed, exemplified knowledge and understanding of:**
>
> • The policies of the main political parties
> • Extent to which the policies of the main political parties differ
>
> **And** balanced comment on/analysis of the view that there are few policy differences between the main political parties.

Answers may refer to:

- Expect reference to the prescribed areas of education, taxation, Europe and law and order but accept accurate references to other areas of policy difference.
- Differences/similarities in policy can be within or between parties in Scotland or the UK.

Conservatives:

- Budget deficit reduction; growth in the economy.
- Proposed scrapping of GCSE in England; Conservative reforms to education in England and Wales.
- Reduction in 50% tax rate to 45%.
- Renegotiate UK's 'relationship with EU'.
- Individualist approach; aim to reduce taxes/State spending; priority to reduce debt.
- Other: Reform of NHS in England and Wales (opposed by Labour).

Labour:

- Opposition to 'granny tax'; demands to close tax loopholes.
- More collectivist approach.
- Emphasis on growth in the economy and job creation.
- 'The UK at the heart of Europe'.
- Opposition to 'free schools' in England.

Liberal Democrats:

- Priority of increasing the personal tax allowance to more than £10,000.
- Reduce class sizes, increase spending on education, commitment to phase out tuition fees in England and Wales.
- Greater use of alternatives to prison.
- Opposition to nuclear weapons.
- Support for UK involvement in a reformed EU.

Scottish National Party:
- Independence for Scotland.
- Opposition to nuclear weapons.
- Council Tax freeze.
- No tuition fees, support for Modern Apprenticeships.
- Increased use of alternatives to prison.
- Since 2010, Conservative and Liberal Democrat coalition in Westminster. In Scotland parties are in opposition.
- Credit similarities and differences in policy within and between parties in relation to the 2011 Scottish Parliament elections.
- Other relevant points.

Question A4

Study Theme 1D: Electoral Systems, Voting and Political Attitudes

> **'Pass' and better answers should feature developed, exemplified knowledge and understanding of:**
>
> - The main features of the STV and First Past the Post
> - The extent to which STV provides fairer representation than FPTP
>
> **And** balanced comment on/analysis of the view that STV provides fairer representation than FPTP

Main features of STV (used in Scottish local government elections since 2007)
- Multi-member wards; voters rank candidates in order of preference; voters may cast vote within and between parties; voters can vote for as few or as many candidates as they like.
- Voters choose within parties rather than party lists.
- More likely power shared between parties; compromise politics. Coalitions are more likely. In 2012, only 5 Scottish Councils controlled by single party, 27 council areas are either coalitions or no overall control.
- Every vote counts; no 'wasted votes'; votes of equal value; no tactical voting; leads to results that are a more accurate reflection of the voter's wishes.
- SNP largest number of councillors.

Claim that STV provides 'fairer representation'
- Choice of locally elected representatives.
- No tactical voting; no wasted votes, every vote counts.
- Overall result is roughly proportionate to percentage of votes cast for each party therefore delivering fairer representation.
- Smaller parties are more likely to gain representation eg Greens have 16 councillors across Scotland, over 200 Independent councillors elected.
- Less likelihood of single party councils; coalitions more likely which, arguably, leads to fairer representation.
- Greater representation of female candidates with 2012 returning the largest proportion of female councillors since current councils established in 1995.

Main Features of FPTP (UK Parliamentary elections)
- Single candidate representing constituency which retains direct MP/Voter link and arguably offering better representation than multimember council wards.
- Established, simple and straightforward; candidate with most votes win seat. Largest party forms Government.
- Arguably, easier to dismiss unpopular Government.

Claim that FPTP provides 'fairer representation'
- FPTP usually leads to a clear winner and strong, stable government that delivers fairer representation.
- Close constituency-representative link.

- Usually one party wins majority in government (except 2010); no compromise politics or coalitions that no one voted for.
- Winner takes all with largest party given the opportunity to carry out their manifesto pledges without having to compromise and dilute their policies with coalition partners (except 2010).
- FPTP harder for smaller parties to gain representation but 2010 saw first Green MP elected as well as single issue candidates and Independents in previous elections (George Galloway, Dr Richard Taylor).
- STV more likely to result in power shared between parties; coalition more likely. In 2012, only 5 Scottish Councils controlled by single party. 27 council areas are either coalitions or no overall control.
- Other relevant points.

Question B5

Study Theme 2: Wealth and Health Inequalities

> **'Pass' and better answers should feature developed, exemplified knowledge and understanding of:**
>
> - Aims of the UK's Welfare State
> - Extent to which the Welfare State continues to meet its aims
>
> **And** balanced comment/analysis on the extent to which the UK's Welfare State continues to meet its aims

Answers may refer to:
- Welfare State- a system of social protection with the state taking the lead role in caring from 'cradle to grave'.
- Designed to tackle the 'Five Giant Evils' (squalor, ignorance, want, idleness and disease) with creation of NHS, development of education services, expansion of social housing and introduction of greater social security coverage.
- Flat rate contributions; universal benefits.
- In terms of NHS and healthcare: aims to be universal, comprehensive, free at 'point of need', high quality. Success of NHS: increases in life expectancy, lower death rates, wide range of high quality services, etc. Balanced by- waiting lists and waiting times, hospital infections, staff shortages, food quality, growth in private healthcare, etc.
- Rises in pensioner and child poverty after several years of progress; wide range of benefits to many groups including elderly, children, those with disabilities balanced with impact of Coalition welfare policies since 2010- Universal Credit, cuts in benefit, cap on housing and other benefits; 'bedroom tax', scrapping of tax credits.
- Increased use of food banks.
- Success of NHS- lower death rates; longer life expectancy, etc but continued problems eg shortages of staff/resources/equipment etc.
- For education, provision from nursery to university level; specialised provision; rising number of university graduates; improvements in primary and secondary attainment. Balanced by: university fees in England and Wales; international comparisons, numbers leaving school with no qualifications, shortages of staff and educational materials, cuts in education spending, etc.
- Quality and availability of council house, end of right to buy, growing number of homelessness; council house waiting lists.
- Differences through devolution: no tuition fees, 'free personal care', no prescription charges, eye tests, bus passes balanced by on-going debate regarding affordability of universal benefits and calls by Scottish universities for fees

or graduate tax. Legislation extending housing entitlement to 'end' homelessness.

- On-going debate of affordability of 'free' personal care in Scotland; plans to reform social services/limit State expenditure elsewhere in the UK.
- Coalition Government claim they meet fundamental principles of a welfare state as they support those "genuinely in need". Beveridge did not intend to support those wilfully choosing a life of welfare dependency.
- Cameron's 'Big Society'.
- 'Breadline Britain' report March 2013
- Other relevant points.

Question B6

> **'Pass' and better answers should feature developed, exemplified knowledge and understanding of:**
>
> - Government legislation or policies to reduce gender and/or race inequalities
> - Success or otherwise of government policies or legislation to reduce gender and/or race inequalities
>
> **And** balanced comment/analysis on the view that the UK government has failed to reduce gender and/or race inequalities

Answers may refer to:

- 2010 Equality Act. This consolidates all previous equalities legislation. The Act includes:
  - Employers being able to take 'positive action' to recruit groups that are under-represented in their workforce.
  - Public sector employers to publish pay audits showing differences between male and female employees. This requirement is voluntary for private sector.
  - Workers must be paid the same for work of 'equal value'.
  - The Equalities and Human Rights Commission monitors and supports the Equality Act.
- The full time gender pay gap at historic low (11.9% in Scotland), however the Chartered Management Institute reported that it would not be until 2067 that pay equality would be achieved.
- 'Sex and Power' report highlighted that 'glass ceiling' for top jobs still remains; women make up 26.2% in politics; 26.1% in public sector; 15.1% in media and culture and 10.2% in business. Women predominately work in the '5 Cs'.
- However, more women in high status professions than ever before. Many examples of successful women eg E Angiolini (former Lord Advocate), Lucy Scott Moncrieffe (VP of Law Society), Michelle Mone etc.
- Rise in number of female small business owners however women affected disproportionately by Coalition's benefit changes. Women still more likely to suffer poverty, 30,000 women sacked per year for being pregnant.
- 2 million workers benefit from NMW – 75% of them women or ethnic minorities.
- 2010 government report 'Tackling Race Inequality: Statement on Race' acknowledged progress in tackling racial inequality in UK. Success of initiatives such as Ethnic Minority Employment Task Force and Black Pupils Achievement Programme.
- Range of initiatives to promote racial equality, eg One Scotland Campaign.
- In 2008, 16% of 18-24 year old ethnic minority population in higher education compared to 14.2% of general population.
- Poverty rates for Asian British (particularly Bangladeshi and Pakistani) and Black British higher than White British. Median earnings for White British a third higher than for Asian British.

- Unemployment rates higher for ethnic minorities (14% compared to 7%). Figure for 2013 much higher for 18/24 age group (black unemployment rate of 45% compared to white rate of 19%). This considered a factor in Tottenham riots and subsequent disturbances.
- Other relevant points.

Question C7

Study Theme 3A: The Republic of South Africa

> **'Pass' and better answers should feature developed, exemplified knowledge and understanding of:**
>
> - Evidence of inequalities
> - Extent to which inequalities are greater within racial groups than between racial groups
>
> **And** balanced comment/analysis on the view that inequalities are greater within racial groups than between racial groups.

Answers may refer to:

- Reference may be made to income/wealth/poverty levels, employment/unemployment rates, housing, education, health and healthcare and crime.
- Creation of Black Middle Class (the 'Cappuccino Society') and Black elite ('Black Diamonds').
- Estimated 450,000 whites, of a total white population of 4.5 million, live below the poverty line.
- Gini-coefficient figure for Whites is 0.5 for Blacks 0.62, Coloureds 0.61 and Indians 0.6. These figures have widened for all racial groups.
- 1.3 million blacks (14% of the black workforce) earn as much as or more than the average white. In 2000, the average black South African earned 15% of the average white South African's income, whereas in 2011, an average black person earned 40% of an average white person's income.
- The official unemployment rate for Black South Africans in 2012 was 29.1% compared to 23.9% for coloureds, 9.3% for Indian/Asians and 6.1% for Whites.
- 2013 report by South Africa Institute of Race Relations found:
  - Number of employed black people doubled since 1994; ratios of 1:3.3 black employed / unemployed.
  - There are three times more black, coloured and Indian business owners than there are white business owners.
  - Black people who own cars has doubled in eight years.
  - 5.8 million black people own their own property.
- The average white person's income is currently rising by 5.3% a year, whereas the average black person's income is rising by 14.9%.
- Based on the national definition of poverty- $4 a day- more than half of South Africans (54%) are poor and poverty and inequality still reflect race.
- Former chairperson of the South African Human Rights Commission, Judge Jody Kollapen, says that South Africa remains one of the most unequal societies in the world.
- Criticism that BEE as benefited only a few Black South Africans ('Black Diamonds') eg mining magnate Patrice Motsepe- whose wealth is estimated at about Rs14.2 billion (US$2 Billion)- and ANC housing minister Tokyo Sexwale.
- Credit also references to geographic and urban-rural inequalities where they are linked to race.
- Overall, inequalities have reduced between different racial groups but have increased within racial groups.
- Other relevant points.

Question C8

Study Theme 3B: China

> **'Pass' and better answers should feature developed, exemplified knowledge and understanding of:**
>
> • Evidence of economic success
> • Extent to which all Chinese people have benefited
>
> **And** balanced comment/analysis of the view that economic success has benefited all the people of China.

Answers may refer to:

• China has developed a 'socialist market economy' over the past 30 years. China has second largest economy after USA with increases of around 9.5% pa.
• The International Monetary Fund states the country's GDP has rocketed from just over $200 billion in 1980 to $5.9 trillion in 2010 although there are signs in 2012 of a slowdown.
• Development of social security system including unemployment insurance, medical insurance, maternity benefits, communal and individual pensions. Intention is to reduce inequalities.
• 11th Five Year Economic Program aimed to build a more 'harmonious society'. 12th Five Year program targets economic growth (7%pa); more new jobs (45m urban areas) and price stability.
• Regional development plans to improve infrastructure and employment opportunities and to promote private and international investment.
• China's Gini-coefficient has risen to 0.47 passing the USA 0.4 which is seen as high.
• Since economic change introduced, hundreds of millions have been lifted out of poverty. There have been huge improvements in the standard of living for majority although millions continue to experience poverty including many in countryside and migrant workers.
• Average urban disposal incomes are three times that of the average rural disposal income. The gap is widening.
• Widespread social unrest with protests often triggered by inequalities and/or other social problems.
• Creation of rich elite (with very expensive lifestyles). There is also a growing middle class with high levels of personal savings. Wealth concentrated in urban areas especially Beijing and Shanghai.
• The government has targets to: lift further 40m people out of poverty in rural areas; to raise minimum wages for migrant workers; improve rural incomes through tax cuts; ensure greater enforcement of labour laws and is working to move labour-intensive, low value industries to more rural areas.
• Credit references to inequalities in education, health/healthcare, housing and consumption of material/consumer goods, etc.
• Other relevant points.

Question C9

Study Theme 3C – The United States of America

> **'Pass' and better answers should feature developed, exemplified knowledge and understanding of:**
>
> • The US immigration debate
> • The impact of immigration on US society (economic, social, political, cultural)
>
> **And** balanced comment/analysis on the overall impact of immigration on the USA

Answers may refer to:

• Immigration subject to much debate in USA. 9/11 and the introduction of various laws (Patriot Act). Immigration (legal and illegal) remains high on the US political and media agenda. Many Americans now see immigration as no longer an economic issue. Post 9/11, it is now seen as a national security issue.
• Historically, USA has rich history of immigration; ethnic diversity seen as a cause for celebration.
• Immigrants stimulate demand for housing, medical care, education, etc; they provide US businesses with a steady reserve of workers prepared to do low paid, low skilled menial jobs that many US citizens won't do; immigrants vital to the economy in states of high Hispanic immigration such as Texas or California.
• In the longer term, immigrants contribute more than they cost to assimilate. Most are young, economically active and, in many cases, highly skilled; they are less dependent on welfare parents than native born Americans.
• Asian American immigrants, particularly, Korean Americans, now out performing White Americans in terms of academic qualifications and average salary. Many work in high tech computer companies of California's Silicon Valley. It can be argued that Korean Americans are now the most successful ethnic group in the USA.
• Bush's Guest Worker Program attempted to recognise the economic contribution of immigration by allowing US employers to sponsor non US employees. Many businesses support changes in the law that allow illegal immigrants to remain legally in the country.
• 40 million people in the USA are immigrants, with illegal immigration accounting for around 12 million. Around 1.5 million illegal immigrants enter the country each year, mainly across the 2,000 mile US/Mexican border. Many believe this level is unsustainable. However, rates of immigration have fallen in recent years.
• Arguments that wage levels of US citizens are being forced down by immigrants and that increased immigration has led to greater competition for employment, education, healthcare, housing, etc. Acc. to Federation for American Immigration Reform (FAIR), the estimated cost of immigration to the US taxpayer per annum is $100bn.
• Many immigrants lack any formal education. They are unskilled and are seen as a drain on the welfare and other social provisions. This costs the US taxpayer- 33% of immigrants use at least one welfare program, compared to 19% of US citizens.
• In 2013 Senate passed a bill to citizenship for an estimated 11 million undocumented immigrants. Obama looking for 'comprehensive settlement on immigration' but pro-immigration groups claim he has increased rate of deportations.
• Fear of US culture being 'overwhelmed' in areas of concentrated immigration; English no longer main language in some areas. Hispanics predicted to be majority ethnic group in California by 2030.
• Immigration major political issue in states such as Texas, California and Arizona and in 2012 US Presidential election. Arizona's new law in 2010 allows police to check the immigration status of anyone giving 'reasonable suspicion'; increased tensions in areas of high immigrant populations.
• Many Americans welcome tighter border controls. Huge investment in border security (including fence along 2,000 mile US/Mexican border) and the creation of Dept. of Homeland Security implies that illegal immigration and its prevention is seen as major issue by State and Federal authorities.

- Growth of anti-immigrant militia groups, eg The Minutemen.
- Other relevant points.

Question C10

Study Theme 3D – The European Union

> **'Pass' and better answers should feature developed, exemplified knowledge and understanding of:**
>
> - Reform of the Common Agricultural and Fisheries Policies
> - Agreement/disagreement over reforms
>
> **And** balanced comment/analysis of the extent of agreement between EU members over reforms to the CAP/CFP.

Answers may refer to:

Candidates **must** refer to both the CAP and the CFP for full marks.

Maximum 12 if only one dealt with

Reform of CAP
- Reform has centred around the need to:
  - Break the link between subsidies and production.
  - Diversify the rural economy.
  - Respond to consumer demands for safe food and high standards of animal welfare and environmental protection.
- Reform proposals which will come into effect in 2013:
  - Keeping EU farm spending level until 2020.
  - Capping the total subsidy a large farm can receive at 300,000 euros. This is to combat large payments going to affluent landowners.
  - Levelling imbalances in payments. Subsidising acreage farmed rather than production totals. This should lead to less intensive farming. Big disparities between high subsidies to farmers in western EU, and much lower ones to those in the east, should also be levelled out.
  - Ending sugar production quotas. These are seen to heavily disadvantage competing farmers in poor countries; and they pay huge amounts to giant European agri-businesses.
  - Making 30% of the "direct payment" income support payments received by farmers dependent on environmental criteria.

Agreement/Disagreement

For some the proposals have gone too far, for some not far enough.
- The UK wanted CAP spending scaled back much more significantly.
- UK farmers have said the reforms will make the payment system even more complicated.
- On the other hand, Irish farmers have protested over the scale of the cuts.

Reform of the CFP
- The Commission wants reform by January 2013.
- It seeks to end the practice of discarding surplus fish. In future trawlers will have to land their entire catch. This will require better technology to monitor compliance.
- The Commission wants EU governments to switch from subsidising fishing fleets to a more market-driven approach to fishing.
- EU wants to restore all fish stocks to maximum sustainable yield (MSY) by 2015.
- Large fleets will be allocated transferable catch shares, called "concessions", which they will be able to trade, in response to local conditions.
- The Commission says fisheries should be managed on an "ecosystem" basis- there needs to be more flexibility in the

system and more scientific data needs to be collected on a larger number of fish species.
- A new funding mechanism will be set up for 2014-2020 called the European Maritime and Fisheries Fund (EMFF), with a budget of 6.7bn euros (£6bn).
- Part of that fund will help support small-scale coastal fleets.
- Member states will be able to restrict fishing in a zone within 12 nautical miles of the coast, up to the year 2022.

Agreement/Disagreement
- The UK has welcomed the changes saying it will encourage a wider range of fish to be caught.
- Critics have questioned whether quotas will be adhered to. Also whether large fishing fleets will dominate the market.
- Some member states eg Germany are keener than others eg Spain to protect stocks.
- Other relevant points.

Question C11.

Study Theme 3E – The Politics of Development in Africa

> **'Pass' and better answers should feature developed, exemplified knowledge and understanding of:**
>
> - The aid versus trade debate
> - The importance of foreign aid and trade as factors affecting development
>
> **And** balanced comment/analysis of the view that trade is more important than foreign aid in promoting development in Africa.

Answers may refer to:
- Some commentators, notably the African academic, Dambisa Moyo, question the value of aid to developing nations.
- Claim that aid encourages dependency not self-reliance.
- Claim that only free trade can benefit both developed and developing nations.
- However, completely free trade may benefit developed nations more as they could flood developed nations with cheap imported goods, damaging local producers and markets.
- There is a recognition within government, eg DFID, that trade and aid are important but other factors such as good governance, tackling corruption and having good infrastructure are as important in promoting development.
- Critics say that deals such as the EU's Free Trade Agreement and the 'Economic Partnership Agreements' (EPAs) are skewed in favour of developed nations.
- Fair Trade refers to a system which allows farmers in developing countries to get a fair price for the goods they sell abroad. But Fair Trade consists of a small and very specific range of products available to Western consumers. It only benefits the exporters of these products and doesn't improve trade within developing nations.
- The UN Millennium Goals 2012 report shows that due to the global economic recession there has been a drop in aid for the first time in many years and a rise in protectionist trade policies.
- Few countries meet the UN's target of 0.7% of GNI in aid. UK achieved in 2013.
- The Doha trade negotiations were supposed to bring greater opportunities for developing countries to gain from world trade. However, these talks have dragged on for many years without resolution.
- Other relevant points.

Question C12.

Study Theme 3F – Global Security

> **'Pass' and better answers should feature developed, exemplified knowledge and understanding of:**
>
> - NATO role/involvement in helping to secure international peace and security
> - Importance of NATO's role in securing international peace and security
>
> **And** balanced comment/analysis of the view that NATO has an important part to play in achieving international peace and security

Answers may refer to:

- Traditional role of collective security.
- 28 member organisation with others keen to join.
- Peace-making and peacekeeping roles eg Kosovo.
- More recent post 9/11 role of tackling international terrorism.
- "New" roles of combatting human trafficking and illegal arms trade which funds terrorism and/or drugs trade.
- Positive and negative views on NATO's involvement in Afghanistan conflict.
- View that United Nations should be the forum for resolving international crises and not NATO. However, UN divided in Security Council (use of veto), restricted in actions by lack of resources (financial and military).
- Terrorism eg al-Qeada.
- "Rogue states" such as North Korea, Iran which could develop nuclear capacity.
- Unrest in the Middle East eg Syrian conflict.
- Emerging crisis in the Ukraine.
- Resurgent Russia with Putin rearming the country and opposing NATO's eastern "missile defence shield".
- Need for NATO illustrated by support given to Libyan rebels, nation building in Afghanistan and Iraq but divisions within NATO too as many countries will not commit troops and US more concerned with its own defence needs.
- Consequences of US unilateral action.
- Other relevant points.

MODERN STUDIES HIGHER PAPER 2 2014

Question 1

Tanya Palmer states, *"As children get older, year-on-year statistics prove that the number of young people regularly eating five fruits per day decreases."* (lines 10-12: Source A)

Source C1 shows that Tanya is exaggerating as the numbers of children eating 5 fruits per day rises from the 5-7 years age group (7%) to the 8-10 years age group (14%)

Question 2

Source A lines 26-29, Tanya Palmer says, *"Although it is true that the majority of children are of a healthy weight, little wonder more than double the number of children are obese in the most deprived families compared to the least deprived."*

Tanya Palmer is **correct** about the majority of children being a healthy weight (76%).

She is **incorrect**, however, when she says, *"...little wonder more than double the number of children are obese in most deprived families compared to the least deprived."* Source C2 shows 7% of least deprived children are obese compared to 11% of most deprived families are obese which is **not double**.

Question 3

Source B, Calvin McKenzie claims that, *"Funding to reduce inequalities for the early years and young people is already one of Scottish Government's biggest areas of expenditure."*

Source C3 shows Calvin exaggerates as funding to reduce inequalities for the early years and young people is the lowest in the table for each of the years.

Question 4

Source B, Calvin McKenzie says, *"Public opinion may agree that government has a responsibility to promote healthy eating but with child poverty rates predicted to fall in the future there really won't be any need for Fruitstart."*

Source C5 supports his view as 65% agree government has a responsibility to promote healthy eating.

But Source C4 does not support his view as child poverty rates are expected to remain steady in the years ahead.

Question 5

DECISION MAKING EXERCISE

The following will be credited:
- An introduction that indicates an awareness of the role to be adopted
- A style appropriate to a report (sub-headings, chapters, etc.)
- A clear recommendation which developed arguments in support of the recommendation
- Identification of and comment on (rebuttal of) counter arguments provision
- Use of appropriate background knowledge
- An overall conclusion

Arguments for the proposal may feature:
The need for healthier living, issues of affordability and availability of fruit for poorest, pressures of modern life leading to problems of obesity, 'invest funds now, save later'.

Arguments against the proposal may feature:
Waste of money, individual responsibility to eat well, role of welfare state, sports facilities not 'nanny state'.

Development of the following statements as background knowledge is acceptable:

Source A

- "Numerous reports show health statistics in Scotland improving but the health gap between the most and least affluent in society is an embarrassment."
- "Government has a responsibility to reduce health inequalities."
- "As a nation we need to eat and live healthier lives."
- "FRUITSTART, once up and running, will sit alongside a number of Scottish Government initiatives to improve health."
- "…inappropriate lifestyle choices and their impact on health."
- "Forward looking government action has, in other areas, been successful in changing lifestyle choices and improving health."
- "But taken as part of a wide range of government health initiatives."

Source B

- "…another example of unnecessary government spending."
- "In a period of economic restraint."
- "…individual's own responsibility to look after their health."
- "Sensibly, and not before time, the UK Government has already made changes to the benefit system with the aim of reducing the UK's 'dependency culture'."
- "…spirit of the Olympics and Commonwealth Games needs to be supported by quality facilities available for all young people."